GCSE COMPUTER SCIENCE COMPLETE VISUAL NOTES

STRUCTURED REVISION NOTES FOR AQA 9-1 GCSE COMPUTER SCIENCE

H A Billinghurst

A CIP record of this book is available from the British Library

First printed September 2019
Previously published as GCSE Computer Science 9-1 Complete Revision Doodle Notes For AQA by H A Billinghurst (ISBN: 9781689576314)

ISBN: 9781690785699

Independently published by Amazon KDP

To find out more about Holly Billinghurst and this book visit www.TeachAllAboutIT.school

How To Use Visual Notes

Each topic consists of a knowledge organiser and two types of notes for you to create a full set of revision notes.

The first page is a visual page with areas for you to colour in, add short notes and doodles to cover the main areas for each topic.

The second page is a more formal page for Cornell style notes. Complete the second column with more detailed notes on each given key term. These can be used like flash cards by covering the second column.

Later, write a summary of the topic at the bottom.

If you need additional help, free topic introductions for GCSE Computer Science can be found at www.TeachAllAboutIT.school or scan any of the QR codes in the knowledge organisers.

CONTENTS

CONTENTS

CONTENTS

CONTENTS

MY REVISION PLANNER

Step 1

I understand that revision is more than simply reading a book. This plan will help me to focus my time and prepare for my exams without the stress of trying to learn everything overnight.

I know that I can only do my best, and if I gave it my best shot, I'll be proud of the effort that I put in.

If I start to doubt myself, I'll come back and read this page.

I've got this.

Divide your subjects into papers.

Subject	Paper 1	Paper 2	Paper 3	Paper 4
Computer Science	Algorithms	Theory	--	--

What papers do you find challenging? Why is that?

_____

_____

_____

MY REVISION PLANNER

Step 2

When Do I need to Revise?

Which 5 days are you going to revise on?

Monday	Tuesday	Wednesday	Thursday	Friday	Saturday	Sunday

How many hours are you going to revise for each week?
(Total number of exam papers x 1 = hours per week)

How many hours per day are you going to revise for?
(Total hours per week ÷ 5 = hours per day

What time each day will you be studying?
Your study blocks shouldn't be more than 2 hours (e.g. 5pm → 7pm)

Monday	Tuesday	Wednesday	Thursday	Friday	Saturday	Sunday
→	→	→	→	→	→	→
→	→	→	→	→	→	→
→	→	→	→	→	→	→

Cross out any blocks that you don't need
You don't need to fill them all!
Remember FIVE days.

3.1 FUNDAMENTALS OF ALGORITHMS

Use the QR codes to access more information online

DECOMPOSITION

Decomposition is breaking a problem down into smaller (more detailed) sections to make a problem easier to solve.

- Decomposition can help break a program into subroutines or modules

- Reconstructing the program from the decomposed sections is called generalisation

_____
_____
_____
_____
_____
_____
_____
_____

ABSTRACTION

Abstraction is the removal of unnecessary detail to make a problem easier to solve, or a program easier to write and debug.

- Problem abstraction is used during the design of a program

- By abstracting a problem, it is easier to spot similarities with other problems that have been solved before

PSEUDOCODE

Pseudocode is a written form of an algorithm that shows the logic of the program.

- Pseudo means 'not real', so while it looks like code, pseudocode is 'not real code'

- Pseudocode is language independent, which means it can be translated into any programming language

- Pseudocde can show more complex designs than flowcharts by including which loops to use and designing subroutines

- Key words like data types & constructs are written in capitals to make it easier to read

_____
_____
_____

FLOWCHARTS

Flowcharts are a visual way to represent an algorithm They only show the logic of a program, not the constructs.

TERMINATOR — The terminator shows the start & end of the algorithm

PROCESS — A process represents actions taken by the program

DECISION — A decision shows where a condition is tested

INPUT / OUTPUT — Input/Output shows interaction with the user

KNOWLEDGE ORGANISER

SORTING ALGORITHMS

There are many different sorting algorithms that vary in efficiency. Efficient algorithms take less time to run, and use less memory.

- Bubble Sort is a simple sorting algorithm that swaps data in pairs repeatedly until the whole list is sorted
  - It is less efficient than others because of the number of iterations needed
- Merge Sort is a more complex sorting algorithm that divides a list into separate items, then merges them back together
  - It becomes more efficient than bubble sort as the length of the list grows

_____
_____
_____

KEY WORDS

Computational Thinking

Decomposition

Abstraction

Flowcharts

Process

Decision

Terminator

Input / Output

Pseudocode

Bubble Sort

Merge Sort

Linear Search

Binary Search

_____
_____
_____
_____

SEARCHING ALGORITHMS

The two main searching algorithms are linear search and binary search.

- Linear gets its name from 'in a line'
- The search starts at the beginning of the list and looks at the data one by one along the line
- Linear search will stop once the search data is found, or the end of the list has been reached

- Binary search is a type of divide and conquer algorithm. The list is divided in half each time a comparison is made
- Binary search is much more efficient than linear search in larger lists
- For binary search to work, the data in the list must be sorted

_____
_____
_____

DECOMPOSITION

Breaking a problem down into smaller, more manageable chunks.

Decomposition is a type of computational thinking

DECOMPOSE YOUR REVISION!

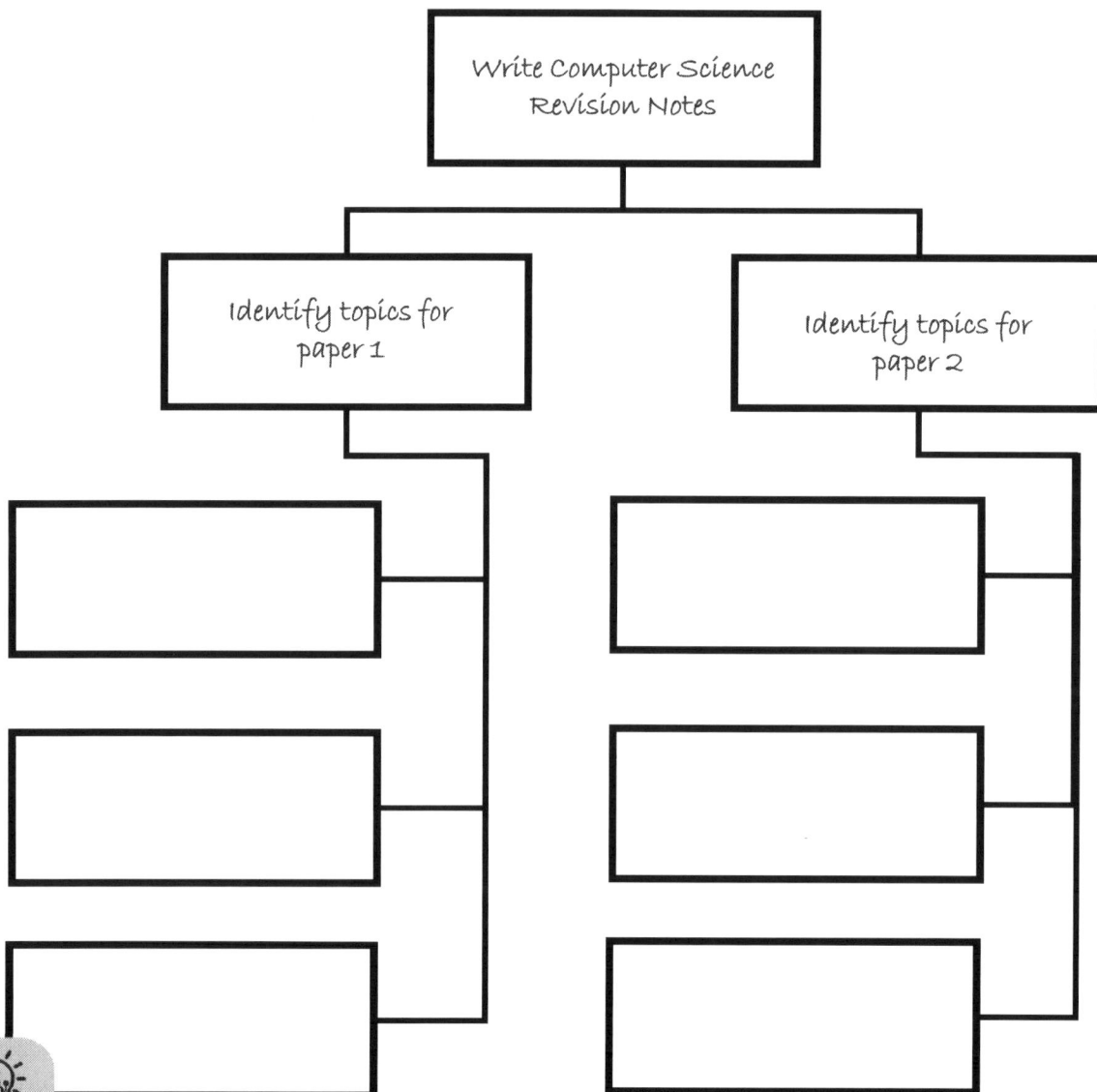

Write Computer Science Revision Notes

Identify topics for paper 1

Identify topics for paper 2

DECOMPOSITION

Key Words	Notes
Decomposition	
Benefits of Decomposition	
Benefits of Modular Code	
Decomposition of making a phone call (example)	Make a phone call

Summary

ABSTRACTION

Abstraction is the removal of unnecessary detail to make a problem easier to solve

This hard drive image is an abstraction – as humans, we see it as a hard drive, but in fact it's just enough detail to allow us to recognize it.

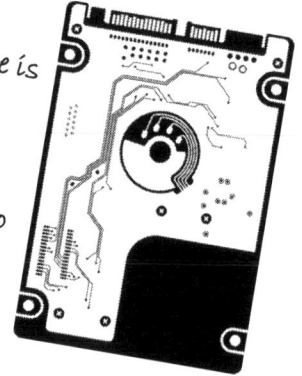

PROBLEM ABSTRACTION

Removing the unnecessary detail to make the problem easier to solve.

PROCEDURAL ABSTRACTION

Removing detail from the main program & placing it into sub-routines

ABSTRACTION IN DATA

Removing unnecessary detail from data structures (e.g. repeating variables) & placing them into more complex data structures (e.g. arrays)

ABSTRACTION

Key Words	Notes
Abstraction	
Problem Abstraction	
Procedural Abstraction	
Abstraction in Data Structures	

Summary

15

FLOWCHARTS

PROCESS

You may be asked to read the logic of a flowchart or write one yourself.

Make sure that you are familiar with how these shapes work together to create logic.

I/O is used for both inputs and outputs. Make sure you use a ruler!

All shapes must be connected using an arrow. If you just use a line, how will you know which way the logic flows?

INPUT / OUTPUT

Decisions are used to show the logic of both SELECTION and ITERATION!

DECISION

A terminator is also called a START/ STOP.

TERMINATOR

Your flowchart should show the logic of your programming CONSTRUCTS: sequence, selection, & iteration.

UNDER CONSTRUCTION

FLOWCHARTS

Key Words	Notes
Process	
Decision	
Input / Output	
Using decisions to represent loops	

Summary

PSEUDOCODE
INPUT / OUTPUT

Pseudocode allows us to represent an algorithm as written logic

INPUT

OUTPUT

Assigning a value to a variable in pseudocode often uses a left pointing arrow ← instead of the = sign

Command	Pseudocode	Example
Output the name "Steve"		
Input your name		
Output the value of the variable name		
Input your age		

PSEUDOCODE EXAMPLE PROGRAM

Example	Pseudocode
Write a program that takes in an integer and outputs all numbers from 1 – the number that divide equally into the input number	

Summary

PSEUDOCODE
SELECTION

Pseudocode allows us to represent an algorithm as written logic

IF, THEN, ELSE

CASE

A CASE statement is an efficient way to represent a long IF, ELSE IF statement

Command	Pseudocode	Example
Output a menu using IF, THEN, ELSE		
Output a menu using CASE		

PSEUDOCODE EXAMPLE PROGRAM

Example	Pseudocode
Write a program that calculates a person's BMI using data that they input into the program. The output should tell them which range they are in according to the standard chart.	

Summary

PSEUDOCODE
ITERATION

Pseudocode allows us to represent an algorithm as written logic

FOR

WHILE

DO UNTIL

Selecting the correct type of loop will help to make your algorithm more efficient

Command	Pseudocode	Example
Output the contents of the following array using a FOR loop: [3,5,2,8,6]		
Ask the user for a password until they enter the word "COMPUTER" using a WHILE loop		
Ask the user for a password until they enter the word "COMPUTER" using a DO UNTIL loop		

PSEUDOCODE EXAMPLE PROGRAM

Example	Pseudocode
Write a program that asks a user to input their age as a whole number. The program should output an error and repeatedly ask for the input until the user enters the correct data type.	

Summary

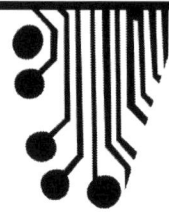

ALGORITHM EFFICIENCY

An algorithm can still meet its criteria without being efficient. Trying other solutions once you've solved the problem can help find a more efficient solution.

For more ideas on how to use re-drafting to improve your work & algorithm design, search for "Austin's Butterfly"

MEMORY EFFICIENCY

An algorithm that saves / duplicates more data than necessary is not efficient

TIME EFFICIENCY

Comparing how long algorithms take to run is the simplest way to compare efficiency

EFFICIENT CONSTRUCTS

Selecting the correct selective statement or iterative loop can help to save time & memory in an algorithm

ALGORITHM EFFICIENCY

Key Words	Notes
Efficiency	
Time Efficiency	
Memory Efficiency	
Use of Constructs	

Summary

SEARCHING

Searching algorithms look for a specific value in a list.

LINEAR

The search is performed in a 'line'

Search "Item"

Position = "Index"

BINARY

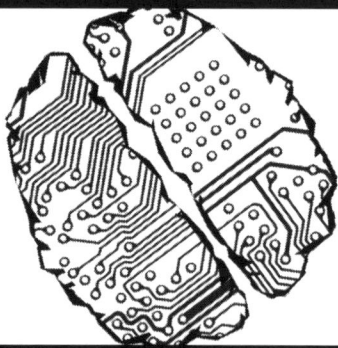

Binary search is called a 'divide & conquer' algorithm

FLAG

A flag is a Boolean value to indicate a true / false value to 'halt' the algorithm.

SEARCHING ALGORITHMS

Complete the algorithms in Pseudocode!

Unsorted Lists

LINEAR

```
List = [3, 7, 9, 2, 5, 10]
search _____
found _____
pos _____

WHILE (found _____) AND (pos < len(List) ) DO
   IF List[pos] _____ search THEN
      found ___ TRUE
   END IF
END WHILE
```

Sorted Lists

BINARY

Binary search is called 'divide and conquer' because each time a loop is executed, the list size halves!

```
List = [3, 7, 9, 2, 5, 10]
search _____
high _____
low _____
mid _____


WHILE (high _____) AND (search _____ List[mid]) DO
   IF search < _____ THEN
      high _____
   ELSE
      low _____
   END IF
   mid ___ (high – low) DIV 2
END WHILE
```

SORTING

Choosing a sorting algorithm depends on the volume of data

More efficient for smaller lists

More efficient for larger lists

BUBBLE

The higher values 'bubble' to the top.

MERGE

Uses recursion to split & merge the lists.

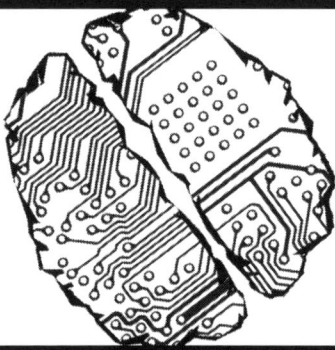

INSERTION

Insertion sort is similar to dropping a stack of papers & putting them back in order as you pick them back up!

SORTING ALGORITHMS

Complete the algorithms
in Pseudocode!

BUBBLE

Bubble Sort uses
'Nested Loops'

swaps _____

WHILE Swaps _____ DO
  FOR I = 0 TO Len(List) -1 DO
    IF List[i] > List[i+1] THEN
      _____ List[i]
      List{i+1] ___ List[i]
      List[i] _____
    END IF
  _____
END WHILE

MERGE

[3, 7, 9, 2, 5, 10]

[3, 7, 9] [2, 5, 10]

[_ , _] [_] [_ , _] [_]

[_] [_] [_]   [_] [_] [_]

[_ , _] [_] [_ , _] [_]

[_ , _ , _] [_ , _ , _]

[2, 3, 5, 7, 9, 10]

INSERTION

FOR i ___ 1 TO Len(List) DO
  pos ___ i
  temp _____

  WHILE List[pos] < List[pos-1]
    List[pos] ___ List[pos-1]
  END WHILE

  List[pos] ___ temp

_____

Merge Sort uses

'Recursion'

29

3.2 PROGRAMMING

DATA TYPES

Programming data types describe the different types of data that can be stored and used within a program.

- An **integer** is a whole number
- A **real** number is a decimal number
- A **string** is one or more characters
- A **character** is a single letter, number, or symbol
- A **boolean** is a special data type that either holds true or false

_____
_____
_____
_____
_____

VARIABLES

Variables are named pieces of memory where the value can change while the program runs.

- The names of variables are declared within the program and are set by the programmer
- Global variables can be seen and accessed anywhere in the program. This makes it easy to overwrite by accident
- Local variables can only be seen and accessed inside their own subroutine. They are more memory efficient & allow the same variable name to be used in different parts of the code without causing an error

PROGRAMMING CONSTRUCTS

Programming constructs describe the building blocks (constructors) of a programming language. By combining these, larger, more complex programs are created.

- **Sequence** is the order in which the lines of code run, or are supposed to run
- **Selection** statements run lines of code only if a condition is met
  - **Iteration** statements allow lines of code to loop based on a logical condition

CONSTANTS

Constants are named pieces of memory where the value cannot change while the program runs.

- Constants are similar, but are not variables
- Using a constant instead of the data allows programmers to easily update repeated data in a program
  - E.g. when tax percentage is changed in a system
  - Missing a single value would cause errors on important calculations

ARITHMETIC & LOGICAL OPERATIONS

Arithmetic operations in programming are used to perform maths functions within a program

+ adds numbers together
- subtracts one number from another
* multiplies one number by another
/ divides one number by another
DIV calculates how many times one number goes into another (integer division)
MOD calculates the remainder after integer division

Logical operations in programming are used to compare data and produce a Boolean (true/false) result

> more than
< less than
>= more than or equal to
<= less than or equal to
== the same as
!= not the same as

SEQUENCE

Sequence is a programming construct that refers to the order in which the lines of code run.

When selection & iteration are added to a program, the sequence becomes more complex as it is no longer linear.

SELECTION

Sequence is a programming construct that refers to the order in which the lines of code run.

- IF, ELSE IF, ELSE statements allow blocks of code to be run when certain conditions are met

- CASE statements are more efficient versions of long ELSE IF statements

ITERATION

Iteration is an alternative name for looping or repeating lines of code

- When the number of iterations is known or can be calculated, a FOR loop is used

  - FOR loops are called count controlled loops & use a variable called a stepper to count how many times the loop has executed

- WHILE loops are condition controlled loops and are used to iterate lines of code until a condition is no longer met

- DO UNTIL loops are condition controlled loops and are used to iterate lines of code until a condition is met

SUBROUTINES

Subroutines are named blocks of code outside of the main program.

- Procedures are subroutines that don't return a value to where they were called

- Functions are subroutines that return a value to where they were called

- Data that is passed into a subroutine inside the brackets is called a parameter

- Using subroutines allows the programmer to reuse the block of code for similar calculations across the whole program

_____

USING FILES

Any data that is entered into a program is lost when the program ends unless it is saved.

- Files allow data to be stored

- Files can be opened in several modes:

  - R – read (get data)

  - W – write (overwrite data)

  - A – append (add to data)

STRING MANIPULATION

Manipulating strings allows us to access each character of the string, take sections out, or simply reverse it.

- The SUBSTRING() function allows a section of a string to be accessed by passing in the starting position and number of characters

- The LEFT() function is like SUBSTRING, but always starts from the first character on the left

- The RIGHT() function is like the LEFT function, but starts from the right & counts backwards

ACCESSING DATA

IT Codes of conduct are rules for an organization (e.g. workplace, school etc) around the proper use of IT equipment

- Codes are usually based around legal use of IT equipment and add extra organizational rules

  - Codes of conduct may also be required as part of belonging to a professional organization such as the BCS (British Computer Society)

KNOWLEDGE ORGANISER

HIGH LEVEL LANGUAGES

- All programming source code needs to be translated into machine code (binary) to allow the computer to process the instructions

- High level programming languages are closer to natural language (the languages used by humans)

- Statements are shorter, but more complex and need to be translated into something the computer can understand

- One high level statement is translated into many low level instructions

_____
_____
_____
_____
_____
_____
_____

LOW LEVEL LANGUAGES

Low level languages, such as assembly language are only a step away from machine code

- Low level languages use mnemonics (shorter logical words) to identify instructions

- Because they are further from natural language, low level languages are more difficult to program

- Low level languages are often quicker to translate and use less memory

- One low level statement is translated into one machine code instruction

Low level languages are often used to program embedded systems

TRANSLATORS

Different translators allow programmers to select an appropriate tool based on how the program is being used

- **Compilers** translate the whole program & create an executable file (.exe) at the end of translation

- **Interpreters** translate the program line by line, and stop if an error is encountered. This can be useful for debugging code and finding syntax errors

- **Assemblers** translate low level languages (assembly language) into machine code

_____
_____
_____
_____
_____
_____
_____
_____

KNOWLEDGE ORGANISER

DATA VALIDATION

Validation allows us to ensure that the data input into a program meets a set of rules.

- Presence checks ensure that the user has input something when prompted (not blank)

- Type checks ensure that the data input matches a specific data type (e.g. integer, string etc.)

- Format checks ensure that the data input matches a set pattern (e.g. DD-MM-YY for a date)

- Range checks ensure that numerical data input is between two numbers

_____
_____
_____
_____
_____
_____
_____
_____

VERIFICATION

Verification allows us to ensure that the data input by the user is what they intended to input.

- Asking a user to enter their new password twice allows the program to check that they match

- Outputting the data entered by the user and asking them to confirm that it is correct is another form of verification

- Outputting a new password to the screen is not appropriate as someone may be able to see – this causes a security risk

TYPES OF TESTING

Testing is not just to find and correct bugs but to ensure that the program works as expected

- The programmer will use **alpha testing** whilst they are writing code to test that the program runs

- Once the program is complete, **beta testing** allows a small group of users early access to give feedback on bugs and usability

- **White box testing** allows the tester to see the program code whilst testing against a set of formal tests

- **Black box testing** requires the tester to perform set of formal tests without access to the program code

_____
_____
_____
_____

KNOWLEDGE ORGANISER

RANDOM NUMBER GENERATION

Random numbers are used in programs to simulate probability.

- All programming languages include a form of built in random function

- Creating a random number requires a lower and upper 'bound' (boundary numbers)

- To create a truly random number, the number is generated as a real number between 0 and 1

- Random numbers can be used to generate password, access item in lists, or simulate games using dice

_____
_____
_____
_____
_____
_____

KEY WORDS

Data Type

Variable

Constant

Construct

Sequence

Selection

Iteration

Boolean Operator

Subroutine

Function

Procedure

File

Record

String Manipulation

Random Number

1D Array

2D Array

ARRAYS

Arrays are special types of variable that can hold more than one value

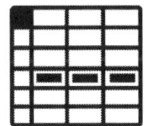

- 1 dimensional arrays are sometimes also called lists

- They can hold more than one item of data, but all data must be the same data type

- The items in a 1D array are accessed by using their position in the list – called an index. E.g. myArray[2]

- 2 dimensional arrays are structured to be like a table

- They can hold more than one row of data, but all data must be the same data type

- The items in a 2D array are accessed using an index for the row & column. E.g. myArray[2][3]

_____
_____

DATA TYPES

Data types tell the computer what form our inputs should take during processing

STRING

Some languages assume all input is a string. Converting to another data type is called 'casting'.

INTEGER

Integers are great for cardinal numbers

REAL

A Real is also sometimes known as a float

CHAR

BOOLEAN

Charles Boole invented the concept of logic using just true or false

DATA TYPES

Key Words	Notes
Integer	
Real / Float	
String	
Char	
Boolean	

Summary

VARIABLES & CONSTANTS

VARIABLES

A variable is a named piece of memory where the value can change as the program runs

Using named pieces of memory allows programs to hold and manipulate data

CONSTANTS

Although a constant is similar to a variable, a constant is NOT a variable

DECLARATION

VAR Name AS STRING

ASSIGNMENT

Name ← "James"

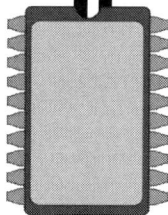

VARIABLES & CONSTANTS

Key Words	Notes
Variable	
Constant	
Meaningful Identifiers	
Declaration	
Assignment	

Summary

SELECTION

Selection is a construct where the code will only run IF a condition is met

IF, THEN, ELSE

ELSE IF can be added to create a secondary condition

CONDITION

This has to be True for the code to run

CASE

CASE is used when a variable may have multiple values

CONSTRUCTS

Think of these like the building blocks of a program.

UNDER CONSTRUCTION

SEQUENCE – SELECTION - ITERATION

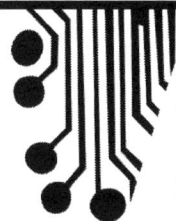

CONSTRUCTS
SELECTION

UNDER CONSTRUCTION

Key Words	Notes
Programming Constructs	
Selection	
IF, ELSE	
IF, ELSE IF, ELSE	
CASE	

Summary

ITERATION

Iteration is a construct where the code repeats until a condition is met

FOR

CONDITION

This has to be True for the code to run

FOR loops repeat a set number of times

WHILE

WHILE loops repeat until a condition is no longer met

The word "Iteration" comes from the Latin word "iter" which means "again"

DO UNTIL

DO Until loops repeat until a condition is met

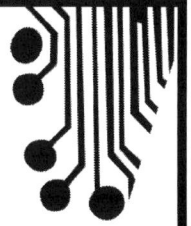

CONSTRUCTS
ITERATION

UNDER CONSTRUCTION

Key Words	Notes
Iteration	
FOR (Count Controlled)	
WHILE (Condition Controlled)	
DO UNTIL (Condition Controlled)	
Stepper / Count controller	

Summary

ARITHMETIC OPERATORS

Arithmetic symbols may differ between pseudocode & your programming language!

BASIC

There are no ASCII symbols for divide & multiply

+

-

/

*

Computers use symbols similar to maths: + - / *

DIV

DIV is used for integer division

MOD

MOD is often used to check for odd or even numbers

Complete the pseudocode for the times table program:

OUTPUT "Enter a number:"
Num ___ INPUT
____ count = 1 ___ 10 ___
   OUTPUT Num ___ Count
   _____

PSEUDOCODE
EXAMPLE PROGRAM

Example	Pseudocode
Write a program that takes in the current time using the 24 hour clock (e.g. "13.01"), then calculates and outputs the time using the 12 hour clock with AM & PM (e.g. "1.01pm".	

Summary

RELATIONAL OPERATORS

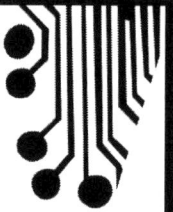

Relational operators will be very similar to the ones that you use in maths.

MORE THAN

\>

\>=

LESS THAN

<

<=

Extend less than by adding "or equal to"

EQUALS

==

!=

Not equal to may also be shown as <>

TIP!
If you're having difficulty with more than less than, make an L with your thumb and forefinger – the one that makes the L shape can also make the 'less than' symbol.

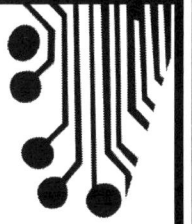

PSEUDOCODE EXAMPLE PROGRAM

Example	Pseudocode
Write a program that takes in a number and triples it. If the result is more than or equal to 10, the program stops and outputs the result. Otherwise, the number is halved and checked again.	

Summary

BOOLEAN OPERATORS

Boolean operators help you to write more complex conditions for selective & iterative statements

Boolean operators are the programmatic version of logic gates

AND

AND will reduce the number of results. useful for ranges.

OR

OR will expand the number of results. useful for condition-controlled loops

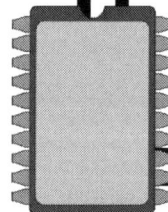

NOT

NOT reverses the condition of a loop

What is the following logic looking for?

WHILE password NOT 'computing' AND password.LENGTH <1 DO
    OUTPUT 'Try Again!'
END WHILE

PSEUDOCODE EXAMPLE PROGRAM

Example	Pseudocode
Write a program that takes in a password as a string. The program should loop until the password is identified as strong: • Is over 8 characters long • Contains lower and upper case letters • Contains a number • And contains a symbol, but not quotation marks	

Summary

1 DIMENSIONAL ARRAYS

Arrays are data structures that can hold more than one item of data

LISTS

We visualize data structures to make them easier for humans to understand. Often 1D arrays are visualized as lists of data

Arrays can be recognized by the use of square brackets []

INDEXES

An index at the back of a book, gives us the position of the word in the book...

PSEUDOCODE

Extend the pseudocode to enter data into the array and output each item

VAR myList AS ARRAY [0 TO 10] of STRING

PSEUDOCODE EXAMPLE PROGRAM

Example	Pseudocode
Write a program that uses a function to validate that each character in a string input by the user exists in a set of characters. The input should be passed in as a parameter & the valid characters should be local variables.	

Summary

2 DIMENSIONAL ARRAYS

2D Arrays are data structures that can hold data in what we see as a table

DECLARATION

Declaring a static 2D array requires you to identify how many rows & columns there will be

2D arrays use two sets of square brackets [][] or [[]]

INDEXES

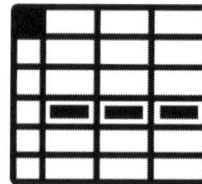

Like the index of a 1D array, the index identifies the individual item using co-ordinates

ROWS

You may find it useful to use the maths rhyme of "Along the corridor, Up the stairs"

COLUMNS

PSEUDOCODE
EXAMPLE PROGRAM

Example	Pseudocode
Write a program that checks a completed Tic Tac Toe board for a winner and outputs which player won the game. A win is three of the same character (O or X) in a row either up, down, or diagonal	

Summary

USING RECORDS FOR DATA

Arrays are not always suitable for holding the data in programs.

RECORDS

Records use names instead of indexes to identify the data they hold

VS. ARRAYS

Arrays are limited to holding one type of data

ARRAY OF RECORDS

To create a table of data, records can be placed into a 1D array to form an array of records

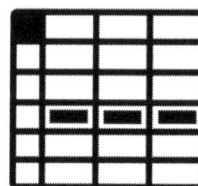

PSEUDOCODE
EXAMPLE PROGRAM

Example	Pseudocode
Write a program that allows the user to enter the following details about their pet and stores it in a record: - Breed - Name - Age - Colour - Weight The program could allow the user to output just one item of data from the record	

Summary

READING FROM & WRITING TO FILES

Files allow us to save data for use after the program has closed

WRITING

Opening a file in write mode deletes all previous data

READING

Opening a file in read mode doesn't allow you to make changes, so keeps the data safer

APPENDING

Appending adds new data to the end of the data that is already saved in the file

When a file is closed, the data is saved.

Much like opening a cupboard door, you can't open it again unless you close it!

PSEUDOCODE EXAMPLE PROGRAM

Example	Pseudocode
Write a program that reads data from a text file called CompTerms.txt Each line of data has two items of data divided by a comma. E.g. **files, programming** The program should organize the data into a 2D array.	

Summary

STRING HANDLING

SUBSTRING()

Substring allows you to access a section of a string by stating the start point & number of characters

Look out for the SUBSTRING() function in your code!

CASTING

Casting allows you to change a variable into a different data type

LEFT( )

Left is like slicing - it returns characters from the left of the string

RIGHT( )

Right is like slicing - it returns characters from the right of the string

STRING HANDLING

Key Words	Notes
String Manipulation	
SUBSTRING	
Casting	
LEFT( ) & RIGHT( )	
Reversing a string	

Summary

RANDOM NUMBER GENERATION

Random numbers are used to create probability within programs

RANDOM

In pseudocode, we pass in the range of numbers as all languages use some form of random function.
e.g. RANDOM(1,10)

PROBABILITY

A roll of a dice can be simulated by creating a random number between the lowest and highest number on the die

PSEUDOCODE

Extend the pseudocode to choose a random item from the list

```
VAR myList AS ARRAY [0 TO 3] of STRING
myList ← ["one player","two player", "quit"]
```

PSEUDOCODE EXAMPLE PROGRAM

Example	Pseudocode
Write a program that simulates a dice game between two players. After each player has rolled their die, the results are matched and the player with the higher score receives points equal to the difference between the dice.	

Summary

SUB-ROUTINES

Creating blocks of re-usable code makes code easier to read, easier to debug, and more efficient

PROCEDURES

A procedure is a type of subroutine that doesn't return a value

FUNCTIONS

A function is a type of subroutine that returns a value to where it was called

APPROPRIATE USE

Example	Subroutine	Pseudocode
Outputting a menu to the user on demand		
Validating user input for a number between 1 & 10		
Writing the user input to a text file after validation		

PSEUDOCODE EXAMPLE PROGRAM

Example	Pseudocode
Write a program that outputs a set of instructions to the user when prompted, then takes in a number and uses a subroutine to validate that it is less than 10. Hint – your program should use 1 function and 1 procedure	

Summary

ACCESSING DATA

PARAMETERS

Parameters are data passed into a subroutine within the brackets

GLOBAL VARIABLES

Global variables can be seen & accessed anywhere in the program

LOCAL VARIABLES

Local variables can only be seen & accessed inside their subroutine

BY VAL / BY REF

By Val passes in the actual data

By ref passes in the reference to the variable

PSEUDOCODE EXAMPLE PROGRAM

Example	Pseudocode
Write a program that uses a function to validate that a number input by the user exists in a set of valid numbers.

The input should be passed in as a parameter & the valid numbers should be local variables. | |

Summary

DATA VALIDATION

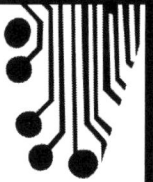

Validation is a check applied to data to ensure that it meets specific rules

PRESENCE

TYPE

RANGE

FORMAT

VALIDATION:

Rule	Validation Used	Test Data
Must be between 0 & 10		
Cannot be blank		
Must be a whole number		
Date must be DD/MM/YY		

DATA VALIDATION

Key Words	Notes
Validation / Verification	
Presence Check	
Range Check	
Type Check	
Format Check	

Summary

TYPES OF TESTING

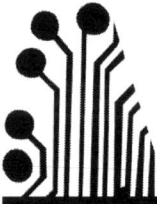

Testing allows us to ensure that the program is bug free and meets the success criteria

WHITE BOX

BLACK BOX

USER ACCEPTANCE

Users test against their original requirements – does the program work as expected?

TEST PLAN TABLES

Complete the testing table!

Test Number	Description	Data	Type	Expected Outcome
1	Enter correct username		Standard	Password prompt appears
2	Enter number instead of username		Erroneous	
3			Boundary	

TYPES OF TESTING

Key Words	Notes
Alpha Testing	
Beta Testing	
White Box Testing	
Black Box Testing	
User Acceptance Testing	

Summary

TYPES OF ERROR

Errors in programs can be categorized in different ways

SYNTAX

Syntax is the spelling & grammar of a language

LOGICAL

Logic errors will allow the code to run, but the output will not be as expected

FATAL

Fatal errors are special logic errors that will cause the program to crash

TIP!
If you're having difficulty finding where the error is in your program, look for the line number in the error message and work upwards through your code (it's often the previous line)

TYPES OF ERROR

Key Words	Notes
Debugging	
Syntax Error	
Logic Error	
Fatal Errors & Using Try / Catch	

Summary

PROGRAMMING LANGUAGES

HIGH

Python

C#

High level programming languages are closer to natural language

All programming languages need to be translated into binary

Low level programming languages are closer to machine language

010
111
1100110
1101101
1100001

LOW

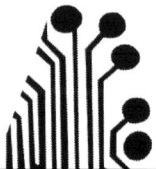

CHOICE OF LANGUAGE

Embedded systems tend to use assembly language – why?

PROGRAMMING LANGUAGES

Key Words	Notes	
Source Code		
High Level Languages		
Low Level Languages		
Choice of Language	High Level Language	Low Level Language

Summary

TRANSLATORS

COMPILER

Compilers produce an executable (.exe) file once completed

INTERPRETER

Interpreters translate high level code line by line

ASSEMBLER

Assemblers translate low level language into machine code

Scenario	Translator	Justification
Debugging Code Syntax		
Distributing a game		
Running code in an embedded system		

TRANSLATORS

Key Words	Notes
Compiler	
Interpreter	
Assembler	
Need for translators in programming	

Summary

3.3 FUNDAMENTALS OF DATA REPRESENTATION

BINARY NUMBERS

Binary uses a base 2 number system – this means there are one 2 unique digits in the system

128	64	32	16	8	4	2	1
0	0	1	0	1	0	1	0

- Binary numbers use **powers of two**
- One **bit** is a single one or zero
- Converting from binary to denary – add up the columns containing a 1
- Converting from denary to binary – put 1s in the columns that are used to add up to the denary number & 0s in the rest

_____
_____
_____
_____
_____
_____

HEXADECIMAL NUMBERS

Hexadecimal uses a base 16 number system – this means there are 16 unique digits in the system.

Hexadecimal uses the same digits as denary (0-9), then represents 10 – 15 as letters.

Hexadecimal is used to represent longer numbers using fewer digits.

10 = A
11 = B
12 = C
13 = D
14 = E
15 = F

_____
_____
_____
_____
_____
_____

BINARY ADDITION

Binary addition uses the same rules as long addition in maths.

$1 + 0 = 1$
$1 + 1 = 10$
$1 + 1 + 1 = 11$

When the answer is longer than the numbers used, this is called overflow

```
  1 0 1 1 0 1
  0 1 1 0 1 1
1 0 0 1 0 0 0
  1 1 1 1 1 0
```

_____
_____

BIT SHIFTING

Bit shifting is used to multiply and divide binary numbers by powers of 2

$0\ 0\ 1\ 1\ 0\ 1 = 13$
$0\ 1\ 1\ 0\ 1\ 0 = 26$

- Shifting left multiplies
- Shifting right divides

_____
_____

KNOWLEDGE ORGANISER

CHARACTER SETS

A character set assigns a number to alphanumeric symbols.

- ASCII is represented using 7 bits
- Unicode is represented using up to 16 bits

- ASCII is represented using 7 bits
- Unicode is represented using up to 16 bits

_____
_____
_____

DIGITAL IMAGES

_____
_____
_____
_____
_____

- Clock speed is the number of FDE cycles that a processor can perform each second

- Clock speed is measured in Hz

- Having multiple cores will improve the speed of the CPU

- A larger cache means more instructions can be held closer to the CPU

SOUND

- General Purpose systems can change what they do by adding more software:. E.g.

  - Desktop PCs / Laptops / Smartphones

_____
_____
_____

COMPRESSION

Compressing data files, allows the memory required to store the file smaller, but keeps the file useable

- Lossy compression removes data making the file lower quality
- Lossless uses an algorithm such as Huffman encoding & Run Length Encoding to compress the data stored and allow the original data to be restored

KEY WORDS

Base

Binary

Hexadecimal

Addition

Bit Shift

Character Set

ASCII

Unicode

Bitmap

Analogue

Digital

Lossy

Lossless

BINARY NUMBERS

2 = BASE 2

The Base of a number system refers to the number of unique digits

DIGITS

0

1

CONVERT

128	64	32	16	8	4	2	1
8	4	2	1	8	4	2	1
0	0	1	0	1	0	1	0

Denary = 32 + 8 + 2 =

You'll need to convert between the number systems without a calculator in the exam!

DENARY

10= BASE 10

Denary is the number system most commonly used by humans!

Why? 10 fingers & 10 toes!

BINARY NUMBERS

Key Words	Notes
Bases	
Denary	
Binary Table	
Converting to Binary	

Summary

HEXADECIMAL

The Base of a number system refers to the number of unique digits

6 + 10 = BASE 16

DIGITS

A
B
C
D
E
F

BINARY

128	64	32	16	8	4	2	1
8	4	2	1	8	4	2	1
0	0	1	0	1	0	1	0

Denary = 32 + 8 + 2 =
Hexadecimal =

Converting via binary may save time without a calculator

TIP!
You may be asked to convert or write out the process for conversions. Make sure you can explain it as well as do it!

DIV & MOD

Identify Denary	150
Divide by required Base	$150 \div 16 = 9.375$
15 DIV 16	=
15 MOD 16	$0.375 * 16 =$
Convert to Hex	

HEXADECIMAL NUMBERS

Key Words	Notes
Hexadecimal Digits	
Converting via Binary	
Converting via DIV & MOD	
Uses of Hexadecimal	

Summary

UNITS OF INFORMATION

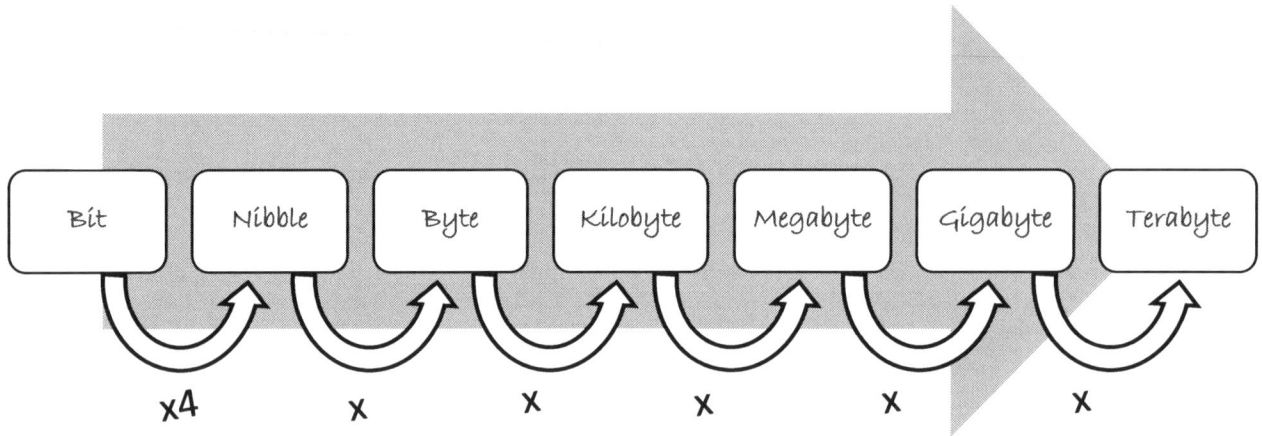

Bit	Nibble	Byte	Kilobyte	Megabyte	Gigabyte	Terabyte

x4   x   x   x   x   x

KB TO TB

How many 104Mb files would fit on a 1Tb drive?

$1 \times 1000 = 1000$ (Tb → ____)
$1000 \times 1000 =$ _____ (Gb → Mb)

$1,000,000$ Mb $/ 104$Mb $=$ _____ files!

A different name is given to capacity using 1024:

KibiByte =

MebiByte =

1024?

FILE SIZES

Different types of file will have different sizes based on the about of data needed.

Average
- Document
- Photo
- Music
- Video

UNITS OF INFORMATION

Key Words	Notes
Bit	
Byte	
Nibble	
Kilobyte	
Megabyte	
Gigabyte	
Terabyte	

Summary

BINARY ADDITION

Adding binary numbers uses the same process as long addition.

RULES

$0 + 0 = 0$

$1 + 0 = 1$

$1 + 1 = 10$

$1 + 1 + 1 = 11$

ADDITION

	0	1	1	0	1	0	1
	1	1	0	0	1	1	0

Denary =

Make sure that you show your carried ones either at the top or bottom of the columns.

OVERFLOW

When adding binary numbers, if the answer is longer than the bit patterns being added, the number will overflow

BINARY ADDITION

Key Words	Notes
Rules of Addition	
Subtraction (extension)	
Overflow	
How CPU deals with Overflow	

Summary

BINARY MULTIPLICATION

Computers cannot multiply or divide directly, but they can apply logic to add numbers together and shift bit patterns left & right

SHIFT LEFT

16	8	4	2	1
0	0	1	1	0

SHIFT RIGHT

16	8	4	2	1
0	0	1	1	0

Only multiplying & dividing by powers of 2 can be achieved by bit shifting

OTHER NUMBERS

Multiplying by other numbers requires a combination of bit shift to the nearest number, then adding

4 * 3 =

	16	8	4	2	1
Shift left by 1	0	1	0	0	0
Add 4	0	0	1	0	0
Binary Addition					

As part of the GCSE, you aren't expected to multiply or divide by numbers that don't use a shift

BINARY MULTIPLICATION

⟵ 0110110 ⟶

Key Words	Notes
Bit Shifting	
Outcome of Shifting Left	
Outcome of Shifting Right	
Numbers that are not powers of 2	

Summary

CHARACTERS

Computers can only represent numbers, so a system was needed to use letters & symbols

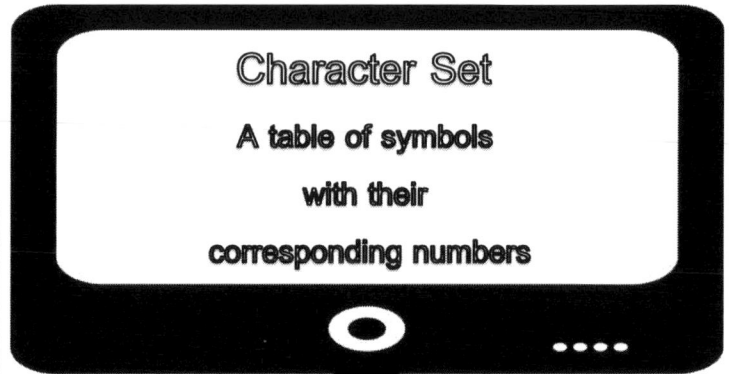

Character Set

A table of symbols with their corresponding numbers

ASCII

ASCII is limited to just the Roman alphabet

You may be asked about the size of ASCII data in the exam in terms of bits & bytes

UNICODE

Unicode has enough space to represent all known alphabets!

USE OF CHARACTERS

Most software will use Unicode as ASCII restricts the use of special characters. However! Unicode requires much more memory.

CHARACTER ENCODING

Key Words	Notes
Character Sets	
ASCII	
Unicode	
Uses of ASCII & Unicode	

Summary

REPRESENTING IMAGES

Bitmap Images use pixels to create a grid of colours making up a more complex image.

A pixel is the smallest addressable area of an image

RESOLUTION

COLOUR DEPTH

Colour depth is the number of bits needed to represent a single pixel

Image resolution & screen resolution are calculated differently

CALCULATING FILE SIZE

Number of pixels x colour depth = number of bits

REPRESENTING IMAGES

Key Words	Notes
Pixel	
Image Resolution	
Colour Depth	
Calculating Image size (memory)	

Summary

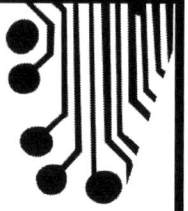

SOUND

We hear analogue sound, but this has to be converted into binary...

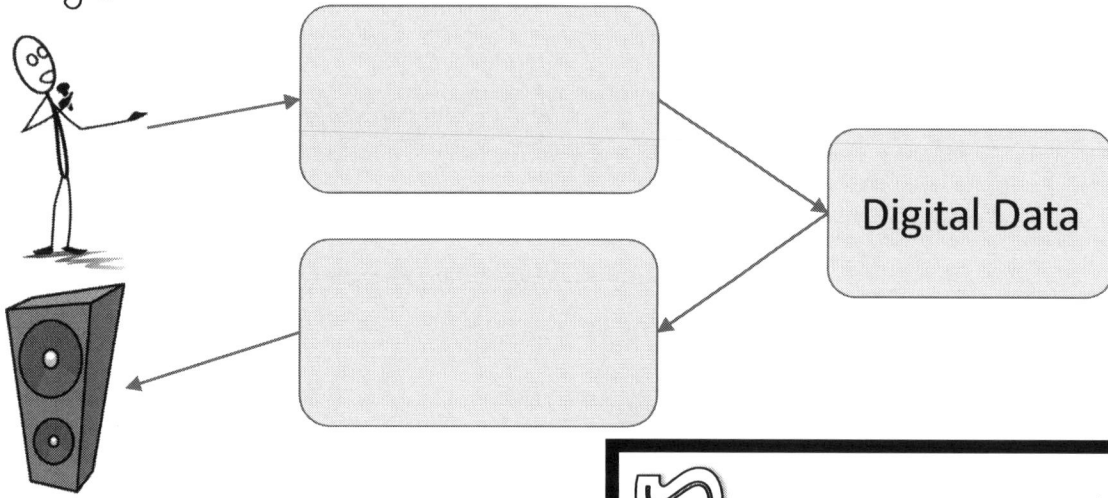

[ ]

[ ]

→ Digital Data

AMPLITUDE & FREQUENCY

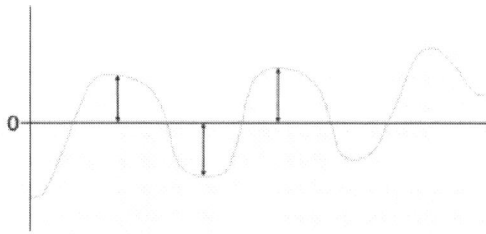

SAMPLES

The height of the wave is measured regularly – this is called a sample

CALCULATING FILE SIZE

Bit Depth x sample rate = bits per second

Bit Depth is similar to colour depth in images. It is the number of bits needed to represent a single sample

REPRESENTING SOUND

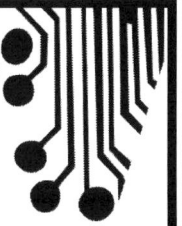

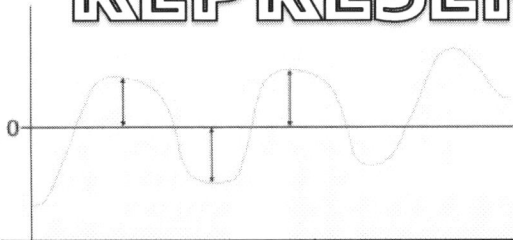

0

Key Words	Notes
Analogue Wave	
Digital Wave	
Amplitude & Frequency	
Sampling	
Calculating File Size	

Summary

COMPRESSION

WHICH ONE?
Will the file be useable after compression?

LOSSLESS

Lossless compression uses an algorithm to save the data in a more efficient format

LOSSY

Lossy compression will remove data which cannot be recovered

If a file needs to be restored back to it's original data for editing, lossless is always best

ZIP

File	Compression Used	Justification
Word Document		
Photograph		
Source Code		
Film for Streaming		

FILE COMPRESSION

Key Words	Notes
Compression	
Lossy	
Lossless	
Suitability of each technique	

Summary

HUFFMAN ENCODING

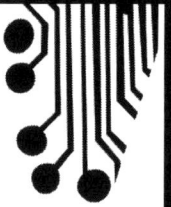

Huffman Encoding is a type of lossless compression for text.

Compression

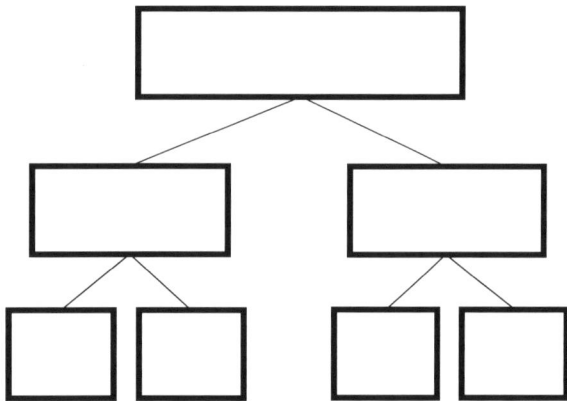

The string 'lossless' has repeated characters so is a good example

BINARY TREES

String "LOSSLESS"

BIT PATTERN

Huffman creates unique bit patterns for each character that can't be confused with another character

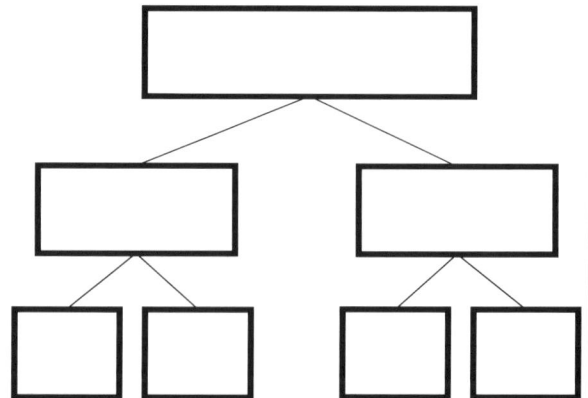

FREQUENCY TABLE

The frequency table is a good way to keep track of which character to add next

The starting table looks like:

O – 1

E – 1

L – 2

S – 4

HUFFMAN ENCODING

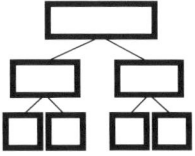

Key Words	Notes
Binary Tree	
Reduced Character Set	
Frequency Table	
Memory Saved by Huffman Encoding	

Summary

3.4 COMPUTER SYSTEMS

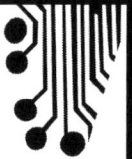

Use the QR codes to access more information online.

RAM VS ROM

Random
Access
Memeory

Read
Only
Memeory

- RAM is volatile (data is lost when power is switched off
- RAM holds currently running programs and data
- Average size of RAM is 4 – 8Gb

- ROM is non-volatile (data is retained when power is switched off
- ROM holds the BIOS & boot up program
- Average size of ROM is 4 – 8 Mb

_____
_____
_____
_____

PURPOSE OF RAM

RAM holds the currently running data and programs.

When the computer is switched on, the BIOS prompts the boot up program to move the Operating System from the hard drive to the RAM.

- RAM has a larger capacity than ROM, but smaller than the hard drive.

- It is fast memory that the CPU can access directly.

- RAM is attached directly to the motherboard in pairs of "sticks"

_____
_____
_____
_____

PURPOSE OF ROM

ROM holds the small programs that allow the computer to start safely.

It is a small chip located on the motherboard, usually close to the CPU.

Like RAM, the ROM can be directly accessed by the CPU.

- ROM holds the BOIS (Basic Input Output System)
  - The BIOS performs a Power on Self Test (POST) when the computer starts

- ROM also holds the Boot Up program that moves the OS to the hard drive

_____
_____
_____
_____

KNOWLEDGE ORGANISER

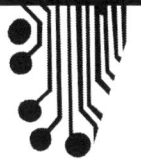

VIRTUAL MEMORY

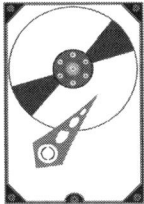

Virtual Memory is used when the RAM is full.

A section of the hard drive is partitioned and used as if it were RAM.

- Data is split into Pages which are moved between the RAM & Virtual Memory
- The lowest priority data is moved to virtual memory
- Virtual memory slows down the CPU as data access is slower

_____
_____
_____
_____
_____
_____

SECONDARY STORAGE

Secondary storage is the term used to describe non-volatile devices used to store data & programs for later use.

- Secondary storage is not directly accessible to the CPU
- Secondary storage is divided into three main types:

  - Optical – E.g. CDs, DVDs, Blu-Ray
  - Magnetic – E.g. HDDs, Floppy Disks, Magnetic Tapes
  - Solid State – E.g. SSDs, USB sticks, SD cards

_____
_____

LOGIC GATES

The CPU processes the logic of instructions using Boolean logic (true or false). We represent this using logic gates & circuits.

AND, OR, and NOT gates are the three basic logic gates. They can be combined to create more complex logic by directing the output of a gate into the input of another.

NAND & NOR gates allow more complex logic to be shown with fewer gates.

XOR is similar to OR but allows 'exclusive' logic

SOFTWARE

Software is the non-physical programs that control the hardware in a computer system

- System software is used to maintain, control, and protect the computer system. This includes operating systems and utility software
- Application software allows the user to complete a task digitally that they could also do offline – e.g. word processor

KNOWLEDGE ORGANISER

Use the QR codes to access more information online.

THE PURPOSE OF THE CPU

Central

Processing

Unit

The CPU is often described as the 'brain' of the computer.

- One CPU can contain many **processors**
- Multiple processors are called cores
- Multiple cores means that more than one instruction can be processed in parallel
- Because some processes need to be linear, not all cores can be used at the same time

_____

_____

_____

_____

_____

_____

OPERATING SYSTEMS

A computer system cannot function without an operating system.

- The OS provides an interface to the user (& hides the complex system)
- The OS provides a platform to install and run other software
- The OS manages hardware and software on the system
- The OS requires additional drivers to manage new peripherals

_____

_____

_____

_____

_____

COMMON CPU COMPONENTS

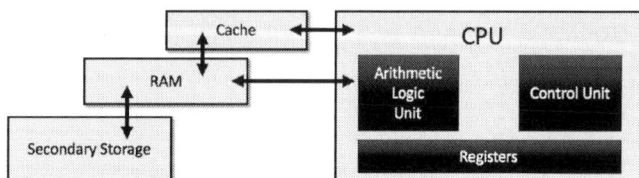

- The Arithmetic Logic Unit (ALU) is responsible for the maths & logic when processing instructions
  - The Control Unit (CU) controls the other CPU components by sending control signals down the control bus

- The Immediate Access Store (IAS) is another term for Primary Memory

- The registers are small pieces of memory inside the processor used to run instructions

KNOWLEDGE ORGANISER

FETCH DECODE EXECUTE

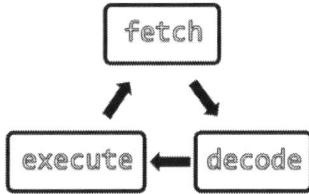

fetch → decode → execute (cycle)

The Fetch Decode Execute Cycle is a set of steps that describe how an instruction is processed in a computer

_____
_____
_____
_____
_____
_____

VON NEUMANN ARCHITECTURE

An architecture is a set of methods & rules to show how a computer processes instructions.

The Von-Neumann architecture is just one type of stored program architecture

Registers are used to store specific data during processing.

Special Purpose Registers:
- PC
- MAR
- MDR
- CIR
- Accumulator

_____
_____
_____
_____
_____
_____

KEY WORDS

Main Memory

Secondary Storage

Virtual Memory

Boolean Logic

Logic Gate

Truth Table

System Software

Application Software

Utility Software

Operating System

Processor

Core

Von-Neumann

ALU

CU

Cache

Register

PC

MAR

MBR

CIR

Accumulator

FDE Cycle

Clock Speed

MAIN MEMORY

Main Memory helps run the computer system.

Volatile

Vs.

Non-Volatile

RAM

R A N D O M

A C C E S S

M E M O R Y

RAM hold the currently running programs and data

ROM

R E A D

O N L Y

M E M O R Y

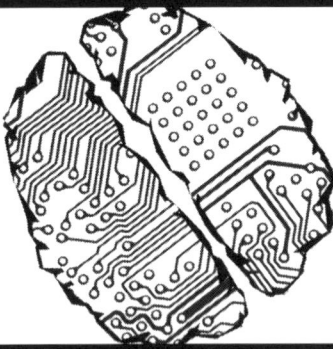

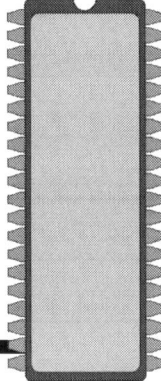

ROM hold the BIOS & Boot Up Program.

CACHE

CACHE can be found inside the CPU (L1) and outside the CPU (L2 & 3)

MAIN MEMORY

Less RAM means fewer programs & data can be held.

PERFORMANCE

RAM & ROM are both built on Flash Memory technology

FLASH

VIRTUAL MEMORY

When the RAM is full, virtual memory helps keep the system running.

Swapping data is called 'Paging'

TYPES OF FLASH MEMORY

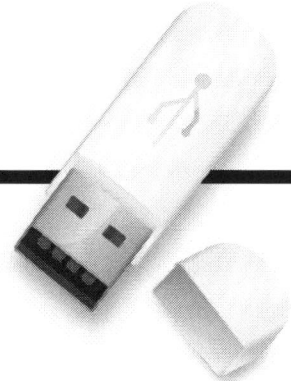

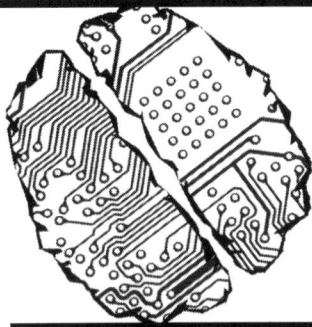

MAIN MEMORY

Key Words	Notes
RAM	
ROM	
Volatile / Non-Volatile	
Characteristics of Main Memory	
Cache	

Summary

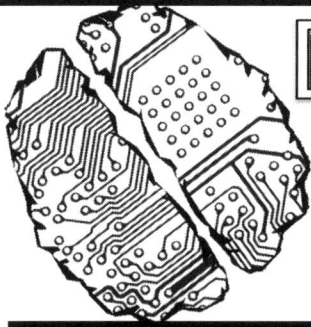

MAIN MEMORY

Key Words	Notes
Virtual Memory	
Pages	
Factors Affecting Performance	
Flash Memory	
Types of Flash Memory	

Summary

SECONDARY STORAGE

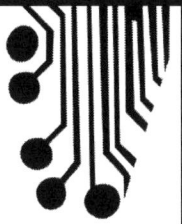

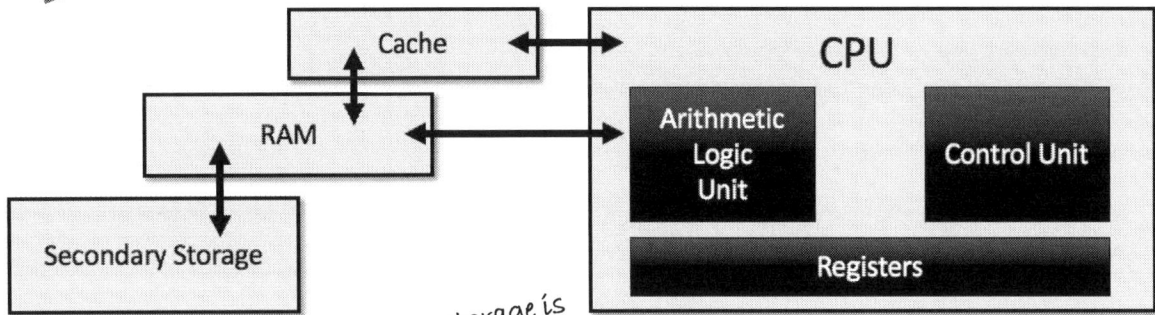

Cache		CPU

Arithmetic Logic Unit

Control Unit

Registers

Secondary Storage

Secondary storage is non-volatile allowing the system to save programs and data.

OPTICAL

Storage that is read by a laser

MAGNETIC

Burn Your Own
Music CD

Holds up to 50 songs!

700 MB
48x Speed
80 min Music

Contents

SOLID STATE

No moving parts = reduced heat

SECONDARY STORAGE

Key Words	Notes
Secondary Storage	
Magnetic	
Optical	
Solid State	
Cloud Storage	

Summary

JUSTIFYING CHOICE OF STORAGE DEVICES

Characteristics are things that help describe an object. Use examples of storage media for each heading.

CAPACITY

How much data can the media hold?

SPEED

How quickly can the CPU access the data?

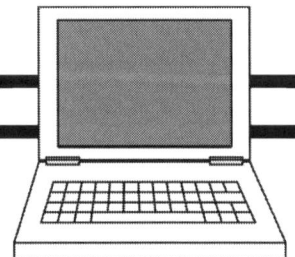

All storage has a purpose and can be compared using six characteristics:
- Capacity
- Speed
- Portability
- Durability
- Reliability
- Cost

PORTABILITY

What happens when you try to use the device on the move?

JUSTIFYING CHOICE OF STORAGE DEVICES

All storage has a purpose and can be compared using six characteristics:
- Capacity
- Speed
- Portability
- Durability
- Reliability
- Cost

What happens if you drop it?

RELIABILITY

Will it open again if needed?

DURABILITY

COST

Not all storage costs the same for the same capacity.

JUSTIFYING CHOICE OF STORAGE DEVICES

Key Words	Notes
Capacity	
Speed	
Portability	
Scenarios where these are important considerations	

Summary

JUSTIFYING CHOICE OF STORAGE DEVICES

Key Words	Notes
Reliability	
Durability	
Cost	
Scenarios where these are important considerations	

Summary

VIRTUAL MEMORY

If the RAM Runs out of space, a portion of the hard drive acts like RAM

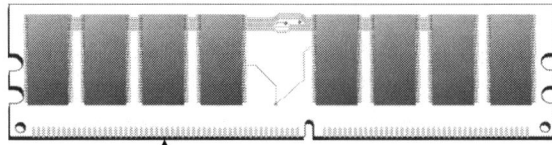

PAGES

Data is moved & held in either pages or segments.

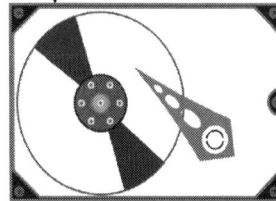

PAGING

Why is my computer slow?

The least important data is placed in virtual. Memory.

DISK THRASHING

Has your computer stopped responding? Check Your CPU usage – it could be Disk Thrashing!

VIRTUAL MEMORY

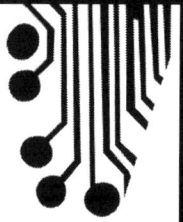

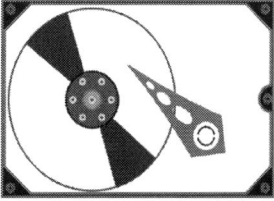

Key Words	Notes
Virtual Memory	
Pages	
Paging	
Why virtual memory affects CPU performance	
Ways to reduce use of VM	

Summary

LOGIC GATES

AND

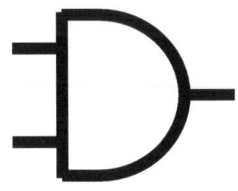

AND gates will only be true if both inputs are true

A	B	C
0	0	
0	1	
1	0	
1	1	

OR

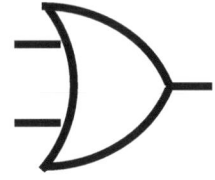

OR gates will only be true if either inputs are true

A	B	C
0	0	
0	1	
1	0	
1	1	

NOT

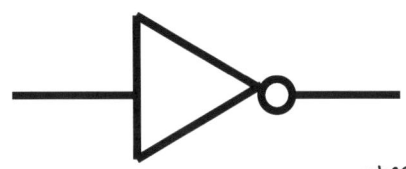

NOT gates reverse the input

A	B
0	
1	

XOR

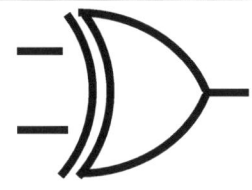

XOR gates will be true if only one input is true

A	B	C
0	0	
0	1	
1	0	
1	1	

NAND

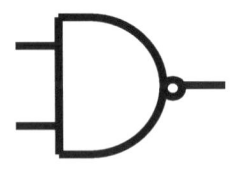

NAND gates are false if both inputs are true

A	B	C
0	0	
0	1	
1	0	
1	1	

NOR

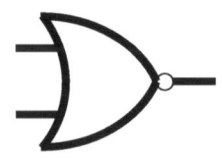

NOR gates are false if either input is true

A	B	C
0	0	
0	1	
1	0	
1	1	

LOGIC CIRCUITS

LOGIC CIRCUITS

By combining logic gates, we can create more complex logic in a circuit

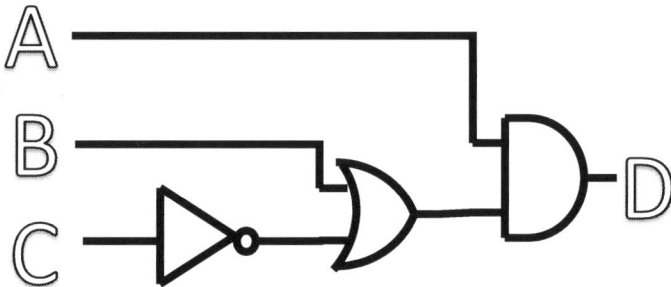

A
B
C
D

TRUTH TABLES

A	B	C	D
0	0	0	
1	0	0	
1	1	0	
0	1	0	
0	1	1	
1	1	1	
1	0	1	
0	0	1	

Truth tables show the potential inputs and logical outputs of a logic gate or circuit.

GREY CODE

Grey Code is an algorithm that helps you to create all possible combinations of input/output

TYPES OF SOFTWARE

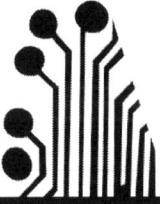

APPLICATION

Application software helps a user perform a task that they could do offline.

SYSTEM

System software helps run, manage, or protect the computer system

COMPARISON:

Software	Application / System	Use
Word processor		
Antivirus		
Operating System		

TYPES OF SOFTWARE

Key Words	Notes
Software	
Application Software	
System Software	
Utility Software	

Summary

OPERATING SYSTEMS

INTERFACE

The operating system hides the complexity of the system.

HARDWARE

The OS manages the hardware of the system through Input/Output controllers

SOFTWARE

The OS provides a platform for other software to run on

DRIVERS

Drivers are small programs that allow the OS to manage new peripherals

A peripheral is an I/O device that connects to the computer system.

OPERATING SYSTEMS

Key Words	Notes
Hardware / Software	
Interfaces	
Drivers	
Cloud Computing (Online Software)	

Summary

UTILITY SOFTWARE

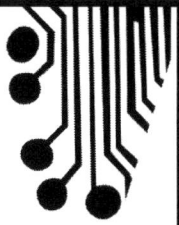

Utility software is a type of system software that manages or protects the system

SECURITY

Security software includes anti-malware & user management software

DIAGNOSTICS

Some software identifies how much memory or processing is required for a task to help identify why the system has slowed

DEFRAGMENTER

Defragmenters reorganize the files on HDD so file data is stored sequentially

Before:

After:

FILE MANAGEMENT

File management allows the user to organize & access files stored on the system

UTILITY SOFTWARE

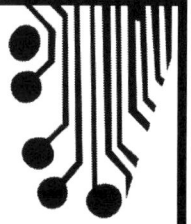

Key Words	Notes
Security	
File Management	
Defragmenters	
Diagnostic Software	

Summary

PURPOSE OF THE CPU

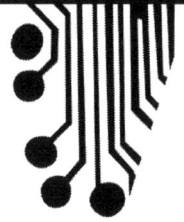

fetch

execute ← **decode**

A clock 'tick' is how long it takes to perform a single FDE cycle

CPU CLOCK SPEED

CPU

The CPU is referred to as the 'brain' of the computer

INSTRUCTIONS

decode
- Opcode
- Operand

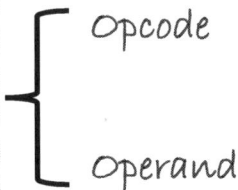

PURPOSE OF THE CPU

Key Words	Notes
CPU	
Fetch-Decode-Execute	
Clock Speed	
Instructions	
Opcode	
Operand	

Summary

COMMON CPU COMPONENTS

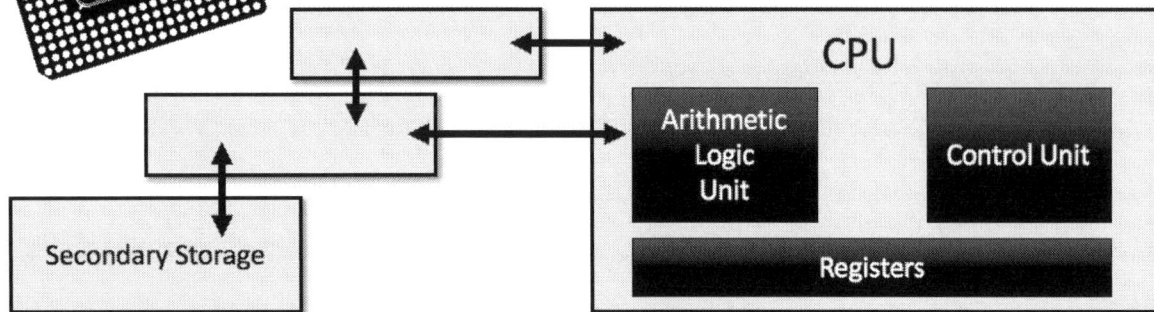

CPU

Arithmetic Logic Unit

Control Unit

Registers

Secondary Storage

CACHE

Main memory is required to run instructions.

ALU

CONTROL UNIT

REGISTERS

PC
MAR
MDR
CIR
Accumulator

PURPOSE OF COMPONENTS

CACHE

Cache is part of Main Memory, but is faster & smaller than RAM

$$\sum_{n=0}^{N-1} e^{-\pi ik}$$
math

CONTROL UNIT

The CU sends control signals using the Control Bus

ALU

Arithmetic & Logic can be seen in high level programming.

BUSSES

Data Bus

Control Bus

Address Bus

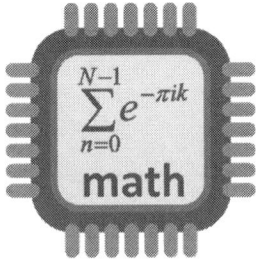

$$\sum_{n=0}^{N-1} e^{-\pi i k}$$

math

Key Words	Notes
Core	
RAM	
Cache	
Control Unit	
ALU	

Summary

$$\sum_{n=0}^{N-1} e^{-\pi ik}$$

math

Key Words	Notes
Busses	
Address Bus	
Data Bus	
Control Bus	
Motherboard	

Summary

SYSTEM ARCHITECTURE

Data & instructions are stored in the same format – Binary!

0110101010

0110

Opcode

1010

Operand

MAR

PC

The Program Counter is the start of the FDE Cycle

MDR

CIR

ACCUMULATOR

THE VON NEUMANN ARCHITECTURE

Key Words	Notes
Architecture	
Register	
PC	
MAR	
MDR	
CIR	
Accumulator	

Summary

FETCH - DECODE - EXECUTE

FETCH

PC

MAR

MDR

Instructions & data are temporarily stored in the cache

DECODE

MDR

CIR

EXECUTE

CIR

ACCUMULATOR

The FDE uses the address bus & the data bus to run the cycle

BUSSES

DATA BUS

CONTROL BUS

ADDRESS BUS

FETCH DECODE EXECUTE CYCLE

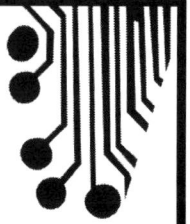

Key Words	Notes
Instruction Set	
Opcode / Operand	
Fetch	
Decode	
Execute	

Summary

FACTORS AFFECTING CPU PERFORMANCE

The speed of the CPU refers to how fast instructions can be processed.

CLOCK SPEED

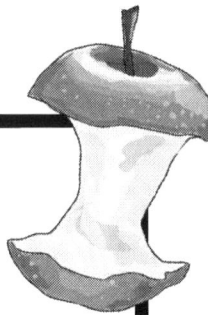

Overclocking refers to increasing the clock speed beyond the recommended limit.

CORES

Doubling the number of cores, does not double the speed!

Calculating the number of instructions:

1Hz =

10MHz =

3GHz =

CACHE SIZE

FACTOR AFFECTING CPU PERFORMANCE

Key Words	Notes
CPU Clock	
Clock Speed	
CPU Cores	
Cache Size	
Overclocking	

Summary

3.5 FUNDAMENTALS OF COMPUTER NETWORKS

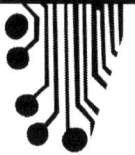

TYPES OF NETWORK

Local **A**rea **N**etwork

Wide **A**rea **N**etwork

Personal **A**rea **N**etwork

- Two or more connected devices create a network
- A LAN is geographically close machines
- A WAN is created by connecting two or more LANs together using telecommunication devices
- A PAN allows wireless devices to connect over a short distance. E.g. smartphone to car stereo

_____
_____
_____
_____
_____

TOPOLOGIES

A topology is the shape of a network.

Devices on a network are called nodes

- Different topologies have different names:

  - Bus – Nodes are connected in a line

  - Star – Nodes are connected through a central node

  - Mesh – All nodes have a connection to all other nodes

_____
_____
_____
_____
_____

NETWORK PROTOCOLS

A protocol is a set of rules that govern data transmission

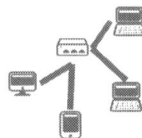

- WiFi is a wireless network protocol called Wireless Fidelity.

- Ethernet is a wired protocol that allows data signals to be sent through a network using copper cables.

- HTTP is the protocol used to send web page data between client & server
- FTP (file transfer protocol) is used to upload files to a web server
- SMTP (simple mail transfer protocol) is used to send email messages
- IMAP (Internet message Access Protocol) is used to download and read email messages on multiple devices

KNOWLEDGE ORGANISER

NETWORK HARDWARE

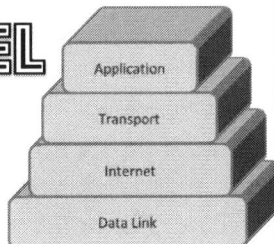

Different devices can perform similar functions. Some are more efficient:

- Router – directs data using an IP address
- Hub – broadcasts data to the network
- Switch – direct data using a MAC address
- WAP – translates wired signals to wireless

_____
_____
_____
_____

THE INTERNET AS A NETWORK

_____
_____
_____
_____

- The internet is the largest form of WAN

- The internet is the hardware – a set of interconnected networks

- The world wide web is the software that allows the internet to function

- The WWW uses the Hypertext Transfer Protocol (HTTP)

TCP/IP MODEL

| Application |
| Transport |
| Internet |
| Data Link |

In order to send data to a device on a network, an address must be used.

- MAC (Media Access Control) addresses are physical & contained on the NIC (Network Interface Card)

- MAC addresses never change

- IP addresses are assigned to the device by the router when the device joins the network

- Because the Router assigns the next available (logical) address to the device, this may change each time the device joins

- The TCP/IP Model is a way of organizing network protocols to show how data packets are created & sent across a network

_____
_____
_____

KEY WORDS

LAN

WAN

PAN

Bandwidth

Bitrate

Media

Client-Server

Peer-2-Peer

SSID

Router

Internet

WWW

Data Packet

TCP/IP

Network Layer

135

TYPES OF NETWORK

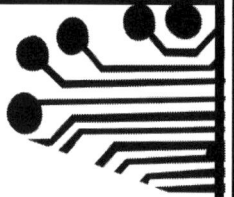

A network is two or more devices connected together to share data and / or hardware

LAN

A LAN may or may not be connected to the internet

WAN

A WAN connects two or more LANs together using telecommunication methods

PAN

What personal devices can you connect together?

MAN

TYPES OF NETWORK

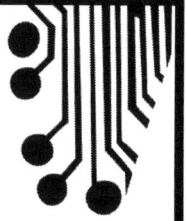

Key Words	Notes
Network	
LAN	
WAN	
PAN	
MAN	

Summary

CLIENT-SERVER VS. PEER-TO-PEER

CLIENT-SERVER

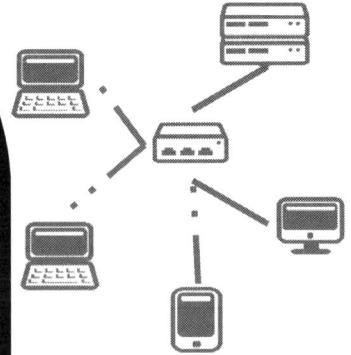

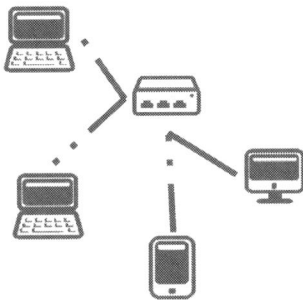

Client-Server networks have a "single point of failure"

PEER TO PEER

In peer to peer, "all nodes are equal"

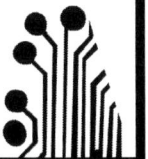

CLIENT-SERVER VS. PEER-TO-PEER

Key Words	Notes
Client-Server	
Peer-to-Peer	
Node	
Benefits / Drawbacks	

Summary

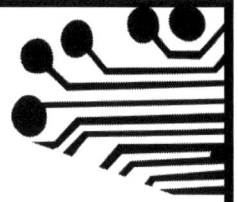

NETWORK HARDWARE

A network is two or more devices connected together to share data and / or hardware

HUB

A hub is the least complex type of routing device.

SWITCH

A switch uses MAC addresses To send data to the correct node

ROUTER

WAP

What other device is often embedded into a router?

140

NETWORK HARDWARE

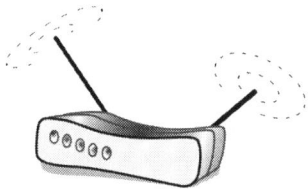

Key Words	Notes
Hub	
Switch	
Router	
WAP	
Media	

Summary

TOPOLOGIES

BUS

A bus topology has a central backbone with each node connected in a line

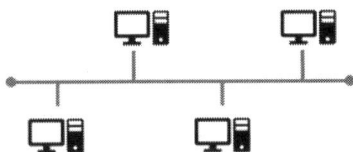

STAR

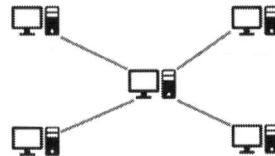

A star topology has a central node with others connected through it. Often this central node is a router or switch

MESH

A mesh topology is set up with every node having a direct connection to every other node.

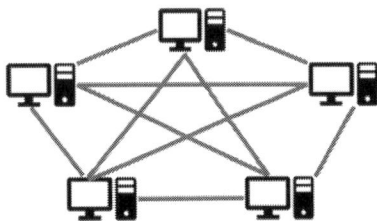

A topology is the shape of a network (either physical or logical).
In modern networks, a combination of more than one topology might be used to create sub-networks. E.g. in a school, a bus might be used along a corridor with each classroom being a star.

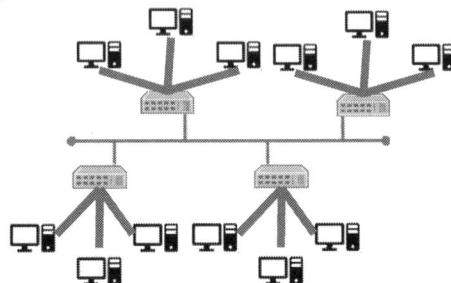

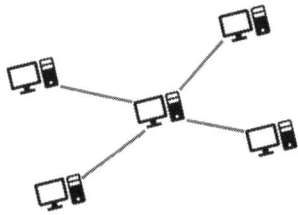

NETWORK TOPOLOGIES

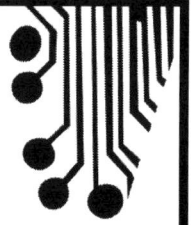

Key Words	Notes
Topology	
Bus	
Star	
Mesh	
Hybrid	

Summary

WIRELESS NETWORKS

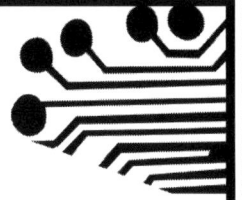

Media is the word used to describe the hardware used to store or transmit data.

WIFI

WiFi is actually a wireless protocol for transferring data using microwaves

SSID

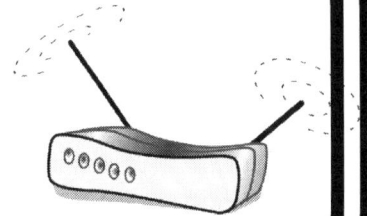

The Service Set Identifier is the name of the Wireless Network

WLAN

A WLAN is a wireless Local Area Network

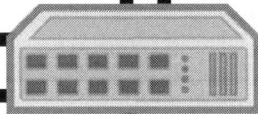

WHITELISTS

Setting a list of allowed devices helps to protect the network

WIRELESS NETWORKS

Key Words	Notes
WLAN	
WiFi	
SSID	
Whitelisting	
Network Hardware	

Summary

NETWORK PROTOCOLS

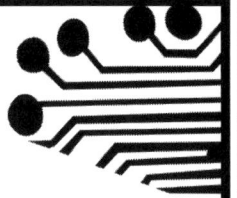

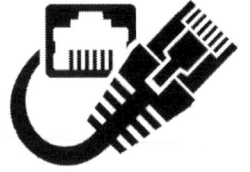

A protocol is a set of rules for the transfer of data between devices

HTTPS

This protocol increases the security of a webpage

SSL

Secure Socket Layer is linked to digital certificates

PORTS

FTPS

A port in a network acts like a door that can be opened or closed

NETWORK PROTOCOLS

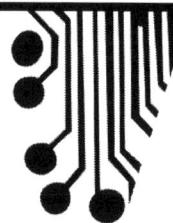

Key Words	Notes
Protocol	
Ports	
HTTP(S)	
SSL	
FTPS	

Summary

NETWORK SECURITY

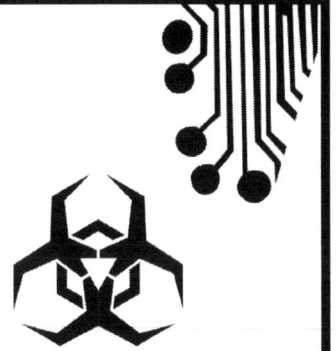

Creating a secure network can help to prevent cyber security threats.

PASSWORDS

Weak passwords are easy to guess, but also put the user at risk from brute force attacks

SOFTWARE UPDATES

Updates are known as patches & contain updates to security features

You may be asked to describe how poor network security may impact data

AUTHENTICATION

3 FACTORS OF AUTHENTICATION

Something I AM

Something I KNOW

Something I Have

NETWORK SECURITY

BIOMETRICS

Writing SLQ into a web form may allow access to the background database

ENCRYPTION

Changing plain text to an unreadable cipher text before sending helps protect data in transit

MAC FILTERING

Banning or allowing only certain devices on a network reduces malicious connections

FIREWALLS

Firewalls can be both software & hardware

Threat	Cause / Explanation
A stranger connecting to your home WLAN	
A malicious connection to your laptop from the internet	
Someone guessing your password	

NETWORK SECURITY

Key Words	Notes
Phishing	
Brute Force Attacks	
Denial of Service Attacks	
Data Interception	

Summary

NETWORK SECURITY

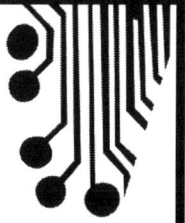

Key Words	Notes
SQL Injection	
Poor Network Policy	
Human Error	
Other Risks	

Summary

PREVENTING VULNERABILITIES

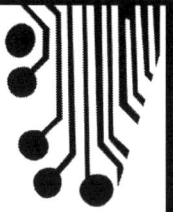

Organisations have a legal obligation to put procedures in place to keep the data that they hold safe

PENETRATION TESTING

Employing users with knowledge of cracking to test how resilient a system helps to put measures in

Data Protection Laws
DPA 1998
GDPR 2018

USER ACCESS LEVELS

User access levels apply to whole folders & systems rather than just files

BACKUP & RECOVERY

Disaster recovery requires a system to store redundant data away from the physical location of the system.

PREVENTING VULNERABILITIES

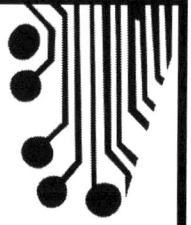

Key Words	Notes
Penetration Testing	
White Hat Hackers	
User Level Access	
Backup & Recovery	

Summary

NETWORK ADDRESSES

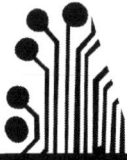

A protocol is a set of rules for the transfer of data between devices

IP ADDRESS

The IP address is assigned as the device joins the network & changes

Both addresses are used to send data over the internet. As a data packet is formed, both addresses are added

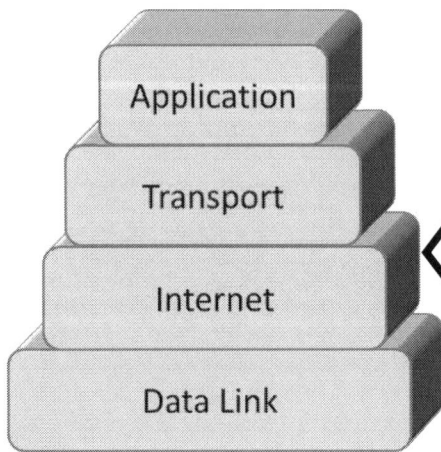

MAC ADDRESS

- Application
- Transport
- Internet
- Data Link

NETWORK ADDRESSES

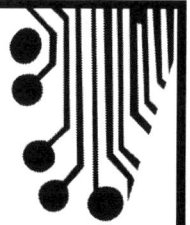

Key Words	Notes
IP Address	
MAC Address	
IPV4 / IPV6	
Logical Address	
Physical Address	

Summary

DATA PACKETS

HEADER

TO: 197.52.68.105
FROM: 127.82.0.197
By: 80
Packet 1 OF 20

DATA

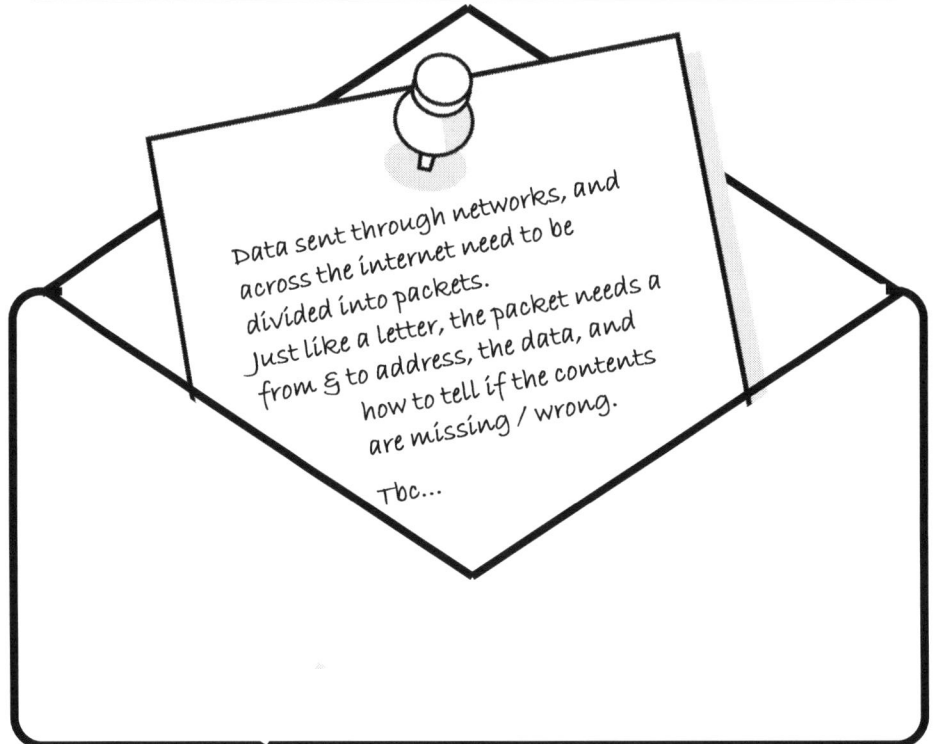

Data sent through networks, and across the internet need to be divided into packets. Just like a letter, the packet needs a from & to address, the data, and how to tell if the contents are missing / wrong.

Tbc...

TRAILER

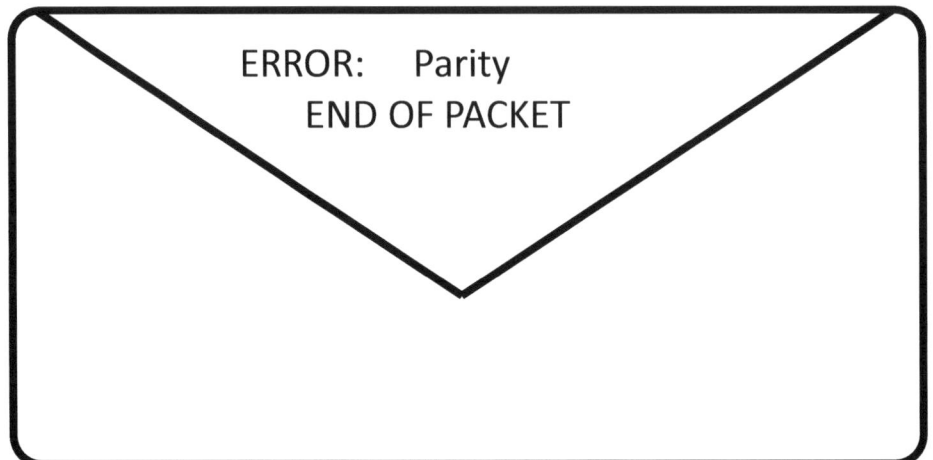

ERROR: Parity
         END OF PACKET

DATA PACKETS

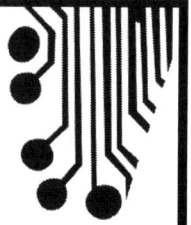

Key Words	Notes
Data Packet	
Header	
Trailer	
Packet Switching	
Circuit Switching	

TCP/IP MODEL

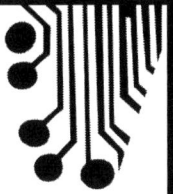

Application Layer

Transport Layer

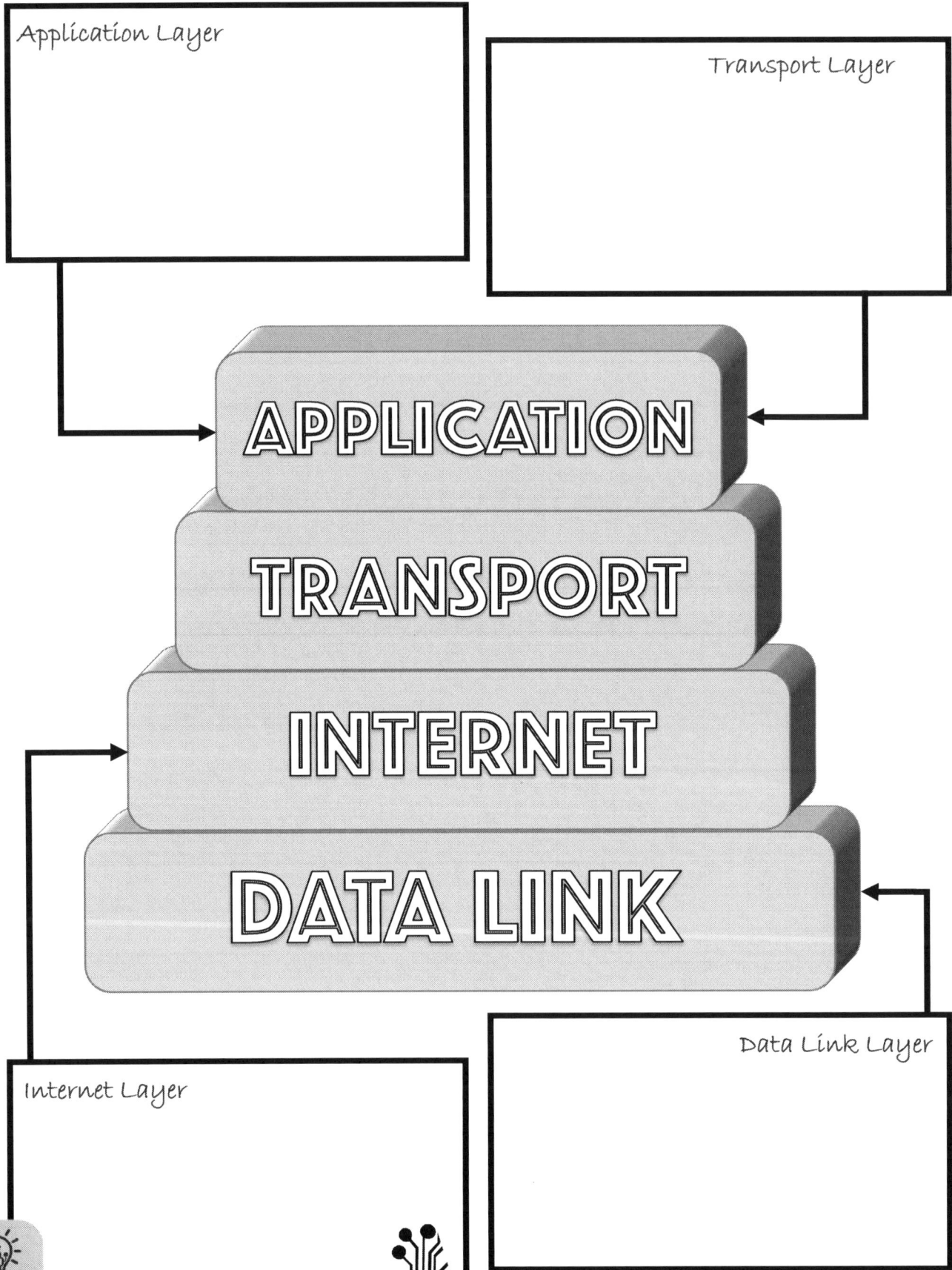

Internet Layer

Data Link Layer

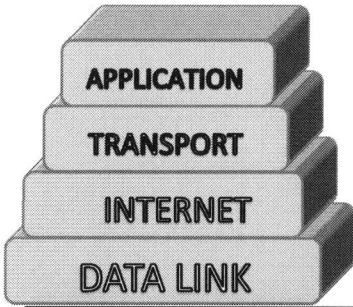

TCP/IP MODEL

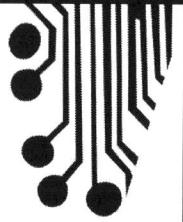

Key Words	Notes
TCP/IP	
Application Layer	
Transport Layer	
Internet Layer	
Data Link Layer	

Summary

3.6 FUNDAMENTALS OF CYBER SECURITY

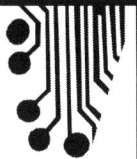

CYBER SECURITY THREATS

Threats may come in the form of direct attacks on a network, or through the introduction of malware into the network.

- Cracking is the act of forcefully accessing a network without permission
- Hacking is the act of forcefully accessing a system and changing or deleting data
- Data can be at risk of theft, deletion, manipulation, or simply human error where data is deleted by accident
- Not every form of attack can be prevented

_____
_____
_____
_____
_____
_____

MALICIOUS SOFTWARE

- **Viruses** replicate themselves and attempt to spread to other devices
- **Worms** are similar to viruses, but can spread without human interaction
- **Spyware** sends data from your machine to the creator of the malware
- A **trojan** is malware that hides inside a gift of non-malicious software
- **Adware** directs you to adverts, or uses your data to show you adverts based on your preferences

_____
_____
_____
_____
_____
_____
_____

SOCIAL ENGINEERING

Social engineering is the act of encouraging someone act in a way they wouldn't usually do.

- Phishing uses emails to manipulate people into sending sensitive data.
- Denial of Service (DOS) attacks create constant requests to the webserver causing the server to become overloaded
  - A brute force attack is a simplistic attack that tries every combination of password to attempt access
  - Data on a network can be intercepted as it is sent. Wireless connections are less secure as they broadcast data

- Typing in a database query into an unprotected webform is called SQL Injection
- Humans are the greatest risks to networ\ks. Having weak network policy allows people to be lazy and adopt bad habits

_____
_____
_____

KNOWLEDGE ORGANISER

PREVENTING THREATS

Organisations have a legal duty to protect the data that they hold under GDPR

- Employing white hat hackers allows a company to test for ways to get into their system using methods that hackers may use. This is called penetration testing

- Setting different access levels for types of user (e.g. teacher / student) allows users to see only the data & programs relevant to them
- Backing up data means taking a copy and placing it in another location. Done regularly, this allows the data that has been lost to be recovered

PROTECTING DATA

- Using strong passwords helps to prevent brute force attacks

- Locking rooms that contain important network devices stops physical theft & data interception

- Network forensics finds the digital footprints of hackers by monitoring network traffic

- Encrypting data on a network means that even if data is intercepted, it is unreadable

- Using firewalls prevents unauthorized access to a network from the internet

- Anti-Malware is a set of programs designed to detect & quarantine malicious software. They must be regularly updated to keep up with new malware

KEY WORDS

Malware
Social Engineering
Virus
Worm
Spyware
Trojan
Adware
Phishing
Brute Force
Interception
DoS / DDoS
SQL Injection
Network Policy
Penetration Testing
User Level Access
Backup & Recovery
Strong Passwords
Physical Access Control
Encryption
Anti-Malware
Firewalls
Auto-Updates

CYBER SECURITY THREATS

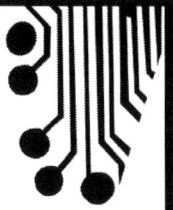

Opening connections to safe users on a network also creates vulnerabilities.

PHISHING

Phishing is associated with email messages, but can also include SMS & internet messages

BRUTE FORCE

This is the least sophisticated method of cracking & is foiled by strong passwords

You may be asked to describe the threats and how to avoid them on a network

DOS

D E N I A L

O F

S E R V I C E

INTERCEPTION

Interception is easier on wireless networks as they may be accessible outside of a building

CYBER SECURITY THREATS!

Threats to networks may be combined with other areas, such as ethics & law to form a longer answer question.
Don't forget to consider how the topics may overlap

NETWORK POLICY

If network policy is poor, loopholes may be created

SQL INJECTION

Writing SLQ into a web form may allow access to the background database

HUMANS

Humans are the biggest threat to any system

Threat	Cause / Explanation
A virus spread through opening an email	
Unable to access website as overloaded	
Private data being leaked about new phone release	

CYBER SECURITY THREATS

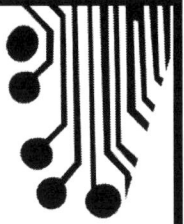

Key Words	Notes
Phishing	
Brute Force Attacks	
Denial of Service Attacks	
Data Interception	

Summary

CYBER SECURITY THREATS

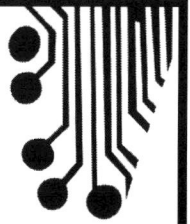

Key Words	Notes
SQL Injection	
Poor Network Policy	
Human Error	
Other Risks	

Summary

Social engineering is the act of making someone behave in a way they might not usually

SOCIAL ENGINEERING

PHISHING

Phishing usually takes the form of an email. When SMS is used, it is referred to as Smishing

PHARMING

Pharming is more sinister as legitimate traffic is forwarded to a spoof website

TARGETED MARKETING

Not all social engineering is malicious. The ethics of how far we want our data to be available for use for these purposes is constantly discussed. The new GDPR rules came about following several high profile uses of personal data.

Tip: Check your social media & browser settings. What access through accounts & cookies do you have allowed?

Many companies use our actions online to send us adverts based on our interests.

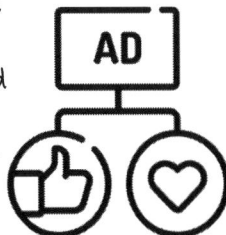

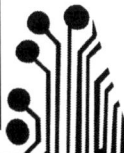

SOCIAL ENGINEERING

Key Words	Notes
Phishing	
Pharming	
Smishing	
Targeted Adverts	
Spoof Websites / News	

Summary

MALICIOUS CODE (MALWARE)

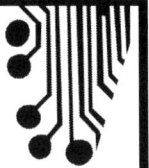

Malware means – "malicious Software" It covers a range of different threats

VIRUSES

SPYWARE

Spyware detects data on a system and sends it back to the creator

You may be asked to describe the difference between types of threats & their solutions

WORMS

Worms are very similar to viruses as they self-replicate, but they can also infect other systems without human interaction.

MALICIOUS CODE (MALWARE)

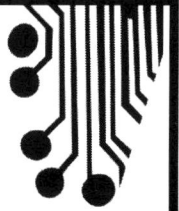

What Should I do?
Investigate ways to Detect & remove Malware

TROJAN

Trojans hide inside other, seemingly harmless software

ADWARE

Adware is often just annoying, but is also a form of spyware used to create targeted adverts

Knowing about threats helps us to investigate methods of protecting devices & networks

Threat	Solution	Justification
Email with a virus accidentally opened		
Ads popping up on screen		
Keylogger found on system		
Free software slows down the computer system		

MALICIOUS CODE (MALWARE)

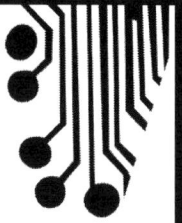

Key Words	Notes
Malware	
Viruses	
Worms	
Spyware	

Summary

MALICIOUS CODE (MALWARE)

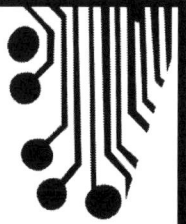

Key Words	Notes
Trojans	
Adware	
Ransomware	
Other malware	

Summary

DETECTING &
PREVENTING THREATS

Organisations have a legal obligation to put procedures in place to keep the data that they hold safe

Data Protection Laws
DPA 1998
GDPR 2018

PENETRATION TESTING

Employing users with knowledge of cracking to test how resilient a system helps to put measures in

USER ACCESS LEVELS

User access levels apply to whole folders & systems rather than just files

BACKUP & RECOVERY

Disaster recovery requires a system to store redundant data away from the physical location of the system.

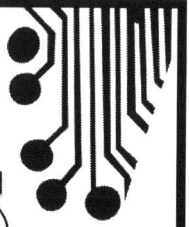

DETECTING & PREVENTING THREATS

Key Words	Notes
Penetration Testing	
White Hat Hackers	
User Level Access	
Backup & Recovery	

Summary

PROTECTING DATA

PASSWORDS

Strong passwords only work if users can remember them.

Protection of data starts with good habits from the people using the network. Strong passwords, user level access, and regular backups & updates

PHYSICAL ACCESS CONTROL

Why is security important?

Who is going into your building? How do you know?

NETWORK FORENSICS

Monitoring the data in a network can help identify hackers and prevent further access.

PROTECTING DATA

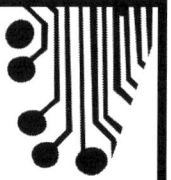

ENCRYPTION

Encryption turns plain text into unreadable text using set algorithms

ANTI-MALWARE

Anti-malware software includes anti-virus, anti-spyware & others

FIREWALLS

Firewalls only allow traffic in & out of the network using agreed ports

Threat	Solution
Hard drives were stolen from a classroom	
Data was intercepted on a network	
A trojan was discovered on a machine	

PROTECTING DATA

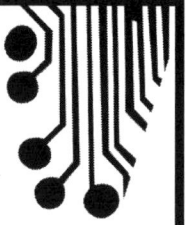

Key Words	Notes
Factors of Authentication	
Strong Passwords	
Physical Access Control	
Network Forensics	

Summary

PROTECTING DATA

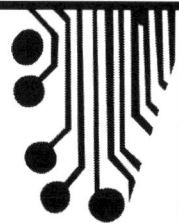

Key Words	Notes
Encryption	
Anti-Malware	
Firewalls	
MAC Address Whitelists	
SSID Hiding	

Summary

3.7 LEGAL, ETHICAL, MORAL, & ENVIRONMENTAL IMPACTS

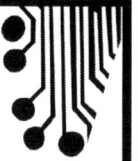

Use the QR codes to access more information online.

ETHICAL COMPUTING

- Morals in computing relate to our personal views on what is right and wrong. These are formed from ethics and laws that we are surrounded by

- Ethics are views on what is right and wrong that are given to us by organisations or the wider society that we live in

- There is overlap between ethics and laws as many laws are made based on society's ethical ideas

_____
_____
_____
_____
_____
_____
_____
_____

- Acting ethically as a company improves trust from users who will be happier to provide their data

- Companies who are unethical may not be breaking the law, but may lose income from sales, and advertising

- An individual's morals may cause them to report an unethical company they are working for. Reporting unethical practice is called whistleblowing

ACCESSIBILITY

There is a legal requirement for developers to make their systems accessible to everyone, including those with disabilities.

- Using accessible coding standards given by W3C helps to make software accessible

    - Alt text on images allows screen readers to describe images

    - Captions on videos & audio transcripts allows people with hearing loss to use multimedia

    - Setting the order or forms (tab index) makes it easier to complete with just a keyboard for people with physical disabilities

CODES OF CONDUCT

IT Codes of conduct are rules for an organization (e.g. workplace, school etc) around the proper use of IT equipment

- Codes are usually based around legal use of IT equipment and add extra organizational rules

    - Codes of conduct may also be required as part of belonging to a professional organization such as the BCS (British Computer Society)

KNOWLEDGE ORGANISER

LEGISLATION

Computing laws are in place to protect data from misuse and sharing without our consent.

- The **Data Protection Act** ensures that organisations keep personal data safe and correct

- The **Computer Misuse Act** is a digital trespass law preventing individuals from accessing systems they don't have authorization for

- The **Freedom of Information Act** allows individuals to request data from public organisations

- The **Copyright & Patents Act** allows creators to protect their designs & intellectual property

- The **Investigatory Powers Act** ensures that public organisations don't infringe on our right to privacy

_____
_____
_____
_____

KEY WORDS

Moral

Ethical

Code of Conduct

Professional Body

Legislation

Data Protection Act 1998

Computer Misuse Act 1990

Investigatory Powers Act

Copyright & Patents Act 1988

Health & Safety Act 1992

Raw Materials in Computing

Carbon Emissions

_____
_____
_____
_____
_____

ENVIRONMENTAL

Computing & technology can have both a positive and negative impact on the environment

- ✓ Algorithms to reduce traffic / find the most efficient route

- ✓ Smart homes using sensors to reduce power consumption

- ✓ Remote collaboration (e.g. VOIP) reducing carbon emission through less travel

- ✗ Additional computers will use more energy

- ✗ Computers use raw materials – not all can be recycled

- ✗ Many components require precious metals that need to be mined (e.g. gold in CPUs)

_____
_____
_____

MORAL & ETHICAL

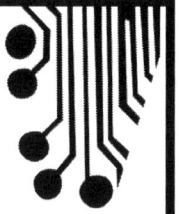

Individual's own ideas of right & wrong

Ideas of right & wrong set by external sources

HEALTH & SAFETY

Are there additional moral or ethical considerations made that go beyond legal requirements?

COPYRIGHT

Theft is legally wrong, but where there are grey areas, how do morals & ethics affect copyright?

COMPUTER MISUSE

Although there are legal rules against computer misuse, what additional moral & ethical rules may apply?

MORAL & ETHICAL

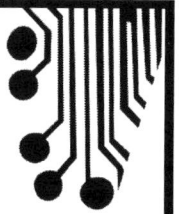

Individual's own ideas of right & wrong

Ideas of right & wrong set by external sources

ACCESSIBILITY

This is for everyone

Many access guidelines are driven by ethics rather than law. Why?

PRIVACY

How would an individual's morals impact on data privacy?

PROTECTION OF DATA

Protection of data is covered by a number of laws. When might these be extended or broken based on moral & ethical considerations?

MORAL & ETHICAL CONSIDERATIONS

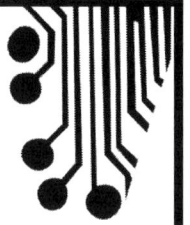

Key Words	Notes
Morals	
Ethics	
Health & Safety (not legal)	
Copyright (not legal)	
Computer Misuse (not legal)	

Summary

MORAL & ETHICAL CONSIDERATIONS

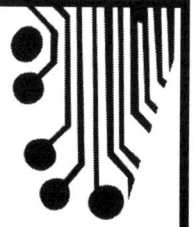

Key Words	Notes
The Digital Divide	
Accessibility	
Privacy	
Protection of Data (not legal)	

Summary

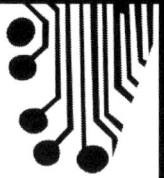

CODES OF CONDUCT

Codes of conduct are usually set out by professional bodies that individuals become members of. In IT, the professional body is called the BCS (British Computer Society)

BENEFITS

Benefits to the individual:

Benefits to the client (or potential clients)

PROFESSIONALISM

Professionalism benefits everyone by setting a minimum standard of quality in an industry.

EXAMPLE: CHECKATRADE

What impact does Checkatrade have on the industry that it promotes? Why?

CODES OF CONDUCT

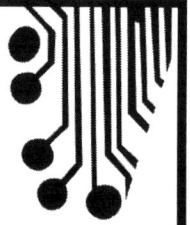

Key Words	Notes
Code of Conduct	
Professional Ethics	
Professionalism	
Benefits of Professional Membership	

Summary

LEGISLATION

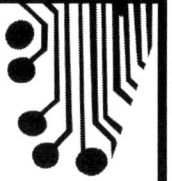

How Do These Laws
Protect Users & Their Data
From Attach & Misuse?

DATA PROTECTION ACT 1998

The DPA was recently replaced by GDPR. Both apply to the organisatiom

COMPUTER MISUSE ACT 1990

The CMA has three levels – why was the legislation brought in around 1990?

INVESTIGATORY POWERS ACT

The Police & Justice Act relates to the Computer Misuse Act in one section. How?

LEGISLATION #2

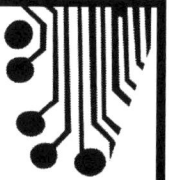

How Do These Laws Protect Users & Their Data From Attach & Misuse?

COPYRIGHT & PATENTS ACT 1988

Copyright enables individuals to protect their intellectual property. How do licenses allow this?

HEALTH & SAFETY REGULATIONS 1992

Health & Safety has specific rulings on Display Screen Equipment

COPYRIGHT REGULATIONS 1992

How does this differ from CPA 1998?

CONSUMER RIGHTS ACT 2015

What consumer rights do you have for hardware / software?

LEGISLATION IN COMPUTING

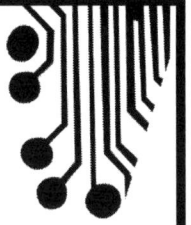

Key Words	Notes
Data Protection Act	
GDPR	
Computer Misuse Act	
Investigator Powers Act	

Summary

LEGISLATION IN COMPUTING

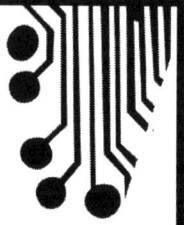

Key Words	Notes
Copyright & Patents Act	
Health & Safety Regulations	
Copyright Regulations	
Consumer Rights Act	

Summary

189

ENVIRONMENTAL IMPACTS OF COMPUTING

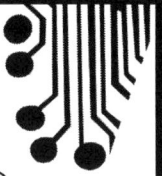

By August 2019, over 150 million computers had been sold across the world in 8 months

ENERGY USE

Computing has both a positive and negative impact on energy use

CARBON EMISSIONS

More people working remotely via the internet provides the potential to reduce carbon emissions

RAW MATERIAL

Computer components use precious metals and plastics that can be recycled or repurposed

ENVIRONMENTAL IMPACTS OF COMPUTING

Key Words	Notes
Energy Use	
Carbon Footprint	
Raw Material	
Smart Homes	
Algorithms for Waste Reduction	

Summary

ACCESSIBILITY

Developers have a legal obligation to ensure that their systems are made accessible.

DISABILITY DISCRIMINATION ACT

What is a 'reasonable adjustment'?

EQUALITY ACT

Equality covers discrimination against any protected characteristic including gender, disability, age, race...

BSI CODE OF PRACTICE

How does this expand on legal obligations?

What guidelines do they provide?

OPEN ACCESSIBILITY FRAMEWORK

ACCESSIBILITY

Sir Tim Berners-Lee created the World Wide Web in 1989. He is the director of W3C and campaigns for the Contract for The Web.

This is for everyone

WHO ARE W3C?

W3 is a shortened version of World Wide Web

WCAG 1.0 & 2.0

What are the Web Content Accessibility Guidelines?

What was changed between 1.0 & 2.0?

UNEQUAL ACCESS

The WWW was set up to allow equal access to information. How do they encourage this?

ACCESSIBILITY

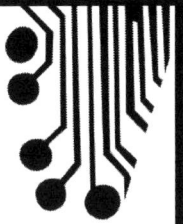

Key Words	Notes
Accessibility in Computing	
Disability Discrimination Act	
Equality Act	
BSI Code of Conduct (British Standards Institute)	
Open Accessibility Framework	

Summary

ACCESSIBILITY IN COMPUTING

Key Words	Notes
World Wide Web Consortium (W3C)	
Web 1.0 vs 2.0	
Accessibility features in Operating Systems	
Digital Divide - Accessibility	

Summary

Printed in Poland
by Amazon Fulfillment
Poland Sp. z o.o., Wrocław